Praise for *When Tear*

'A comprehensive and richly resou
a great team and how to do it. Bac ...... research,
and brightly illuminated with memorable quotes from elite sports
coaches to Michelin star chefs.'

Doris Sew Hoy, accredited executive coach and
author of Trust Yourself First: Cultivating Healthy
Relationships

'*When Teams Work* is a fantastic guide to every aspect of teamwork,
including highly pertinent and important topics such as virtual team
working and how to be truly inclusive. From addressing the bedrocks
of building trust and ensuring psychological security, this book also
illustrates how to resolve conflicts and increase performance. Whether
you are leading, managing, building, coaching or training a team, this
guide has everything covered. Highly recommended!'

Guy Mansfield, Vice-President Finance,
Gas Trading, Total Energies

'Full of practical and useful tips and ideas for anyone who works in,
with or leads a team. Definitely one to add to your bookshelf.'

Siobhan McManamy, Director of Markets,
Tourism Ireland

'If you work in or lead a team, then this is a book you'll want to read.
It's packed with tools, techniques and loads of examples. Practical,
interesting and wide-ranging.'

Dr Samantha Davies, General Practitioner and
Clinical Director, Sarum North PCN

'A book which gives a great insight and understanding of what genuine teamwork looks like and needs. The different elements covered by each chapter give the reader a comparative measure of where an emerging team can be and the value of what needs to be in place as it develops. Great team understanding involves everyone and respects everyone. This is a book to which you will consistently return.'

Sir Ian McGeechan OBE, former Scottish International and British and Irish Lion; coach of several Premiership teams, coach of Scotland and head coach of the British and Irish Lions

WHEN TEAMS WORK

Pearson

At Pearson, we believe in learning – all kinds of learning for all kinds of people. Whether it's at home, in the classroom or in the workplace, learning is the key to improving our life chances.

That's why we're working with leading authors to bring you the latest thinking and best practices, so you can get better at the things that are important to you. You can learn on the page or on the move, and with content that's always crafted to help you understand quickly and apply what you've learned.

If you want to upgrade your personal skills or accelerate your career, become a more effective leader or more powerful communicator, discover new opportunities or simply find more inspiration, we can help you make progress in your work and life.

Every day our work helps learning flourish, and wherever learning flourishes, so do people.

To learn more, please visit us at **www.pearson.com/uk**

The Financial Times

With a worldwide network of highly respected journalists, *The Financial Times* provides global business news, insightful opinion and expert analysis of business, finance and politics. With over 500 journalists reporting from 50 countries worldwide, our in-depth coverage of international news is objectively reported and analysed from an independent, global perspective.

To find out more, visit **www.ft.com**

Mike Brent
Fiona Elsa Dent
Nigel Melville

WHEN TEAMS WORK

HOW TO DEVELOP AND LEAD A HIGH-PERFORMING TEAM

Pearson

Harlow, England • London • New York • Boston • San Francisco • Toronto • Sydney
Dubai • Singapore • Hong Kong • Tokyo • Seoul • Taipei • New Delhi
Cape Town • São Paulo • Mexico City • Madrid • Amsterdam • Munich • Paris • Milan

PEARSON EDUCATION LIMITED
KAO Two
KAO Park
Harlow CM17 9NA
United Kingdom
Tel: +44 (0)1279 623623
Web: www.pearson.com/uk

First edition published 2022 (print and electronic)
© Pearson Education Limited 2022 (print and electronic)

The rights of Mike Brent, Fiona Elsa Dent and Nigel Melville to be identified as authors of this work have been asserted by them in accordance with the Copyright, Designs and Patents Act 1988.

The print publication is protected by copyright. Prior to any prohibited reproduction, storage in a retrieval system, distribution or transmission in any form or by any means, electronic, mechanical, recording or otherwise, permission should be obtained from the publisher or, where applicable, a licence permitting restricted copying in the United Kingdom should be obtained from the Copyright Licensing Agency Ltd, Barnard's Inn, 86 Fetter Lane, London EC4A 1EN.

The ePublication is protected by copyright and must not be copied, reproduced, transferred, distributed, leased, licensed or publicly performed or used in any way except as specifically permitted in writing by the publishers, as allowed under the terms and conditions under which it was purchased, or as strictly permitted by applicable copyright law. Any unauthorised distribution or use of this text may be a direct infringement of the authors' and the publisher's rights and those responsible may be liable in law accordingly.

All trademarks used herein are the property of their respective owners. The use of any trademark in this text does not vest in the author or publisher any trademark ownership rights in such trademarks, nor does the use of such trademarks imply any affiliation with or endorsement of this book by such owners.

Pearson Education is not responsible for the content of third-party internet sites.

ISBN: 978-1-292-27848-3 (print)
      978-1-292-27849-0 (PDF)
      978-1-292-27850-6 (ePub)

British Library Cataloguing-in-Publication Data
A catalogue record for the print edition is available from the British Library

Library of Congress Cataloging-in-Publication Data
A catalog record for the print edition is available from the Library of Congress

10 9 8 7 6 5 4 3 2 1
26 25 24 23 22

Cover design by Two Associates

Print edition typeset in 9.5/13, Helvetica Neue LT W1G by Straive
Printed by Ashford Colour Press Ltd, Gosport

NOTE THAT ANY PAGE CROSS REFERENCES REFER TO THE PRINT EDITION

Mike would like to dedicate this book to the memory of Max Halliwell, a great friend, wonderful neighbour and someone you'd always want on your team.

CONTENTS

Pearson's Commitment to Diversity, Equity and Inclusion

Pearson is dedicated to creating bias-free content that reflects the diversity, depth and breadth of all learners' lived experiences. We embrace the many dimensions of diversity including, but not limited to, race, ethnicity, gender, sex, sexual orientation, socioeconomic status, ability, age and religious or political beliefs.

Education is a powerful force for equity and change in our world. It has the potential to deliver opportunities that improve lives and enable economic mobility. As we work with authors to create content for every product and service, we acknowledge our responsibility to demonstrate inclusivity and incorporate diverse scholarship so that everyone can achieve their potential through learning. As the world's leading learning company, we have a duty to help drive change and live up to our purpose to help more people create a better life for themselves and to create a better world.

Our ambition is to purposefully contribute to a world where:

- Everyone has an equitable and lifelong opportunity to succeed through learning.
- Our educational products and services are inclusive and represent the rich diversity of learners.
- Our educational content accurately reflects the histories and lived experiences of the learners we serve.
- Our educational content prompts deeper discussions with students and motivates them to expand their own learning and worldview.

We are also committed to providing products that are fully accessible to all learners. As per Pearson's guidelines for accessible educational Web media, we test and retest the capabilities of our products against the highest standards for every release, following the WCAG guidelines in developing new products for copyright year 2022 and beyond. You can learn more about Pearson's commitment to accessibility at:

https://www.pearson.com/us/accessibility.html

While we work hard to present unbiased, fully accessible content, we want to hear from you about any concerns or needs regarding this Pearson product so that we can investigate and address them.

- Please contact us with concerns about any potential bias at: https://www.pearson.com/report-bias.html

- For accessibility-related issues, such as using assistive technology with Pearson products, alternative text requests, or accessibility documentation, email the Pearson Disability Support team at: disability.support@pearson

ABOUT THE AUTHORS

MIKE BRENT MA, MSC, DIP MGMT, DIP MKTING, MSC, MCMI

Mike is an Adjunct Member of Faculty and Professor of Leadership Practice at Hult International Business School. He specialises in leadership, team-building, influencing, coaching, cross-cultural management, leading change and personal development. His interests include how to foster self-awareness and creativity, and how to challenge effectively.

With extensive experience as a management trainer, consultant, team facilitator and coach, his interventions include designing and running workshops and seminars and change programmes for organisations in Europe, Asia Pacific, the USA and the Middle East.

Mike studied Sociology and Philosophy at Edinburgh University, where he gained an MA degree. He also has a Diploma in Business Studies, a Diploma in Marketing, a Master's degree in Human Resource Development, and a Master's degree in Organisational Consulting and Change.

Mike holds the British Psychological Society Levels A and B qualification in Psychometric Testing, is a licensed Neuro Linguistic Programming Practitioner and an experienced accredited coach. He is also trained in Solution Focus Therapy and Coaching, and is qualified in a wide range of Psychometric questionnaires including MBTI, FIRO, SDI, Hogan, ESCI, SPM, Lumina Spark and CPI. He has written numerous articles and with co-author Fiona Dent has written five books on leadership, two of which were shortlisted for best practical management book of the year. His books have been translated into Chinese, Arabic, Swedish, Polish, Korean and Japanese. Mike holds both British and French nationalities and is bilingual.

Mike's books: *Influencing – Skills and Techniques for Business Success* (with Fiona Dent) Palgrave Macmillan, 2006); *The Leaders Guide to Influence* (with Fiona Dent) (FT Prentice Hall, 2010); *The Leaders Guide to Managing*

People (with Fiona Dent) (FT Pearson, 2013); *The Leaders Guide to Coaching* (with Fiona Dent) (FT Pearson, 2015); *The Leadership of Teams* (with Fiona Dent) (Bloomsbury, 2016); *Appreciative Leadership* (with Dr Mark McCergow) In *Inspiring Leadership: Becoming a Dynamic and Engaging Leader* (Roger Delves and Kerrie Fleming, eds). (Bloomsbury, 2017).

FIONA ELSA DENT MSC, MA

Fiona is a Professor of Practice for Ashridge Executive Education at Hult International Business School, independent management trainer, executive coach and author. Previously she was a Director of Executive Education at Ashridge and a member of the Ashridge Management Committee, where she was responsible for one of the two education faculty groups that managed programmes and client relationships and delivered management development solutions across Ashridge. Fiona was also involved with her colleagues in setting the strategic direction of the organisation with a particular focus on human resources. She has also worked in the financial services industry and in the local and central government.

Fiona has Programme and Client Director experience, and has worked with a range of organisations and clients on a national and international basis. Recent clients include the BBC, NHS, Easyjet, Abu Dhabi Executive Council, St Gobain and Novartis Pharmaceuticals. Fiona teaches and consults in a broad spectrum of leadership, personal, interpersonal and relationship skills and is trained in a range of psychometrics. Recent coaching clients include a range of senior civil servants, medical and NHS management personnel and a senior manager in the tourism industry.

Fiona has co-authored a range of books including: *Career Agility: Strategies For Success* (Cambridge Scholars Publishing, 2020); *The Leadership of Teams* (Bloomsbury, 2017); *Thrive and Survive as a Working Woman: Your Coaching Toolkit* (Bloomsbury); *The Leader's Guide to Coaching and Mentoring: How to use soft skills to get hard results* (Pearson, 2015); *The Leaders Guide to Managing People: How to use soft skills to get hard results* (Pearson, 2014); *Women in Business: Navigating Career Success* (Palgrave, 2012); *The Leader's Guide to Influence: How to use soft skills to get hard results* (Pearson, 2010); *Working Relationships Pocketbook*

(Management Pocketbooks Ltd, 2009); *Influencing: Skills and Techniques for Business Success* (FT Pearson, 2006); *The Leadership Pocketbook* (Management Pocketbooks Ltd, 2003). She is currently working on a book entitled *Working with Others* with co-authors Viki Holton and Patricia Hind, which will be published in 2022 by Pearson.

NIGEL MELVILLE

Nigel Melville captained the England Rugby team on his debut in 1984, making him the youngest player to captain England on his debut. He also represented the British Lions, Barbarians, the North, Yorkshire, Wasps and Otley. Nigel's international playing career was cut short by serious injury playing for England against Ireland in 1988.

Melville became Head of Promotions for Nike (UK) and started his rugby coaching career with Otley. In 1995 when the game of rugby was professionalised, Nigel became the first full-time Director of Rugby for Wasps, winning the first professional Premiership title in 1996, followed by three National Knock-out Cup appearances, winning two. In March 2002 he moved to Gloucester Rugby, winning the Zurich Championship Final, Powergen Cup and topped the Zurich Premiership table by a record 15 clear points.

In 2006 Nigel worked as a performance consultant to Steve Coppell's Reading F.C., winning the Championship title and being promoted to football's Premiership.

In 2007 Nigel was appointed by USA Rugby as CEO and President of Rugby Operations, where he headed the development of the game for nine years. During this time, membership grew significantly with the award-winning Rugby Rookie programme, introducing the game to thousands of young players across America. Nigel also developed USA Rugby's Olympic Sevens programme based at the Olympic Training Centre in Chula Vista, CA, both men's and women's teams qualifying for the 2016 Olympics in Rio.

He returned to England as Director of Professional Rugby in 2016 supporting the English Professional Clubs and International teams. During this time Nigel lead the development of an Elite Premiership club competition for women and centrally contracting the England Women's team.

In 2020 he was appointed Executive Chairman of the Premiership Rugby Investment Board representing the 13 English Premiership Clubs.

Nigel also works as an Executive Coach with a focus on Executive/ Leadership Development and Team Coaching. His professional development during the last five years has included a Diploma in Professional Coaching Practice, executive coach training and certification. He is an active member of the International Coaching Federation (ICF).

Nigel has always been involved in teams, both in sport and business, as a team member, leader and coach. All teams are unique, but they all share certain traits that can ultimately make the difference between success and failure. In this book, we share with you our experiences of working with teams in sport and business, identifying those critical traits that drive success and explore successful team performance in a variety of other team environments including hospitality, aviation, medicine and more.

AUTHORS' ACKNOWLEDGEMENTS

We would like to acknowledge the help of the hundreds of team members and team leaders that we have spoken to while researching this book. We would specifically like to acknowledge the help and support of our colleagues at Hult International Business School/Ashridge, especially the research team and Sharon West. We are also extremely grateful to our editor at Pearson, Eloise Cook, for her patience, critical eye and support.

As well as those people whose names are mentioned in the book, we are also grateful to the following who read and gave comments on our chapters, or shared their stories with us: Doris Sew Hoy, Will Shorten, Hans Fribergh, William Braddick, Philip Sadler, Professor Mark Mason, Dr Toufik Ftaita, Dr Guy Lubitsch, Rory Hendrikz, Dr Stewart Desson and the team at Lumina, Nicolas Worms, Guy Mansfield, Regan Gallo, Dr Mark McCergow, Lvyi Sheng, Stevie Fine and Katie Stanley at Inspire Training, Liao Jingmei, Koffi Segniagbeto, Michael Chaskalson, Naomi Brown, Jennifer Morris, Philip Last, Pedro Gonzalez, Sylvie Pedar Picard, Drusilla Copeland, Chris Stringer Agnieszka Kolkzarek and Dr Nelisha Wickremansinghe.

Mike would specifically like to thank Dr Muyiwa Ojo Aromokudu for keeping him healthy, Alex Minors and his team for keeping him fit, Ender and his team at Epicure coffee shop, plus Fred & Ginger coffee shop in Berkhamsted for keeping him awake, and his partner Francoise for her support and forbearance. Nigel would like to thank Mike and Fiona for their patience and guidance and for the love and support of his 'special' team, Sue, Helen, James, Tom, Joe and Geordie.

Fiona would like to acknowledge all the teams she has worked in over the years, all of whom have provided ideas and inspiration for many of her contributions to this book. Most importantly the Dent and Davies teams who constantly give her encouragement and insight into how real teams work.

PUBLISHER'S ACKNOWLEDGEMENTS

Text credits:

7 Henry Ford: Quoted by Henry Ford; **8 Harvard Business Publishing:** Parks, S.D. (2005) Leadership can be taught. HBR press; **11 Mark McCergow:** McKergow, M. and Bailey, H. (2014). Host: Six new roles of engagement for teams, organisations, communities and movements. London: Solutions Books. Used with permission from Mark McCergow; **15 Jordan B Petersen:** Quoted by Jordan B Petersen; **20–21 Forbes Media LLC:** Strauss, Andrew: Interview in Forbes magazine. Accessed 20/12/2021 https://www.forbes.com/sites/daniellerossingh/2019/12/19/qa-former-england-captain-andrew-strauss-talks-cricket-business-and-psychology/?sh=72f4bf8a6b39; **27 and 28 Lumina Learning Ltd:** Lumina Learning Ltd © 2022. Used with permissions; **29 Amy C. Edmondson:** Quoted by Dr. Amy Edmondson; **30 David Burkus:** Quoted by David Burkus; **36 Steven Covey:** Quoted by Steven Covey; **38, 47, 87 and 94 Tom Kerridge:** Quoted by Tom Kerridge. Used with permission; **43 Steven Covey:** Quoted by Stephen R Covey; **47 Olivier Sibony:** Quoted by Olivier Sibony; **51 Azeem Rafiq:** Quoted by Azeem Rafiq; **53 Richard Branson:** Quoted by Richard Branson; **56–58 Dr Ghislaine Caulat:** This is from a personal communication with Dr Ghislaine Caulat in 2021. Used with permission; **59 Taylor & Francis Group:** Haslam, Reicher & Platow (2011) The New Psychology of Leadership. Psychology Press; **67 Pearson Education:** Based on Brent, M & Dent, F. (2010) The Leaders' Guide to Influencing. Pearson Education; **70 Thomas Edison:** Quoted by Thomas Edison; **73 Gallup, Inc.:** State of the Global Workplace – Gallup Report (2017); **74 David MacLeod:** Quoted by David MacLeod; **76 and 77 Hult International Business School:** Armstrong, A, Olivier, S. Wilkinson S. (2018) Shades of grey- an exploratory study of engagement in work teams. Ashridge/Hult International Business School; **81 Stephen Covey:** Quoted by Stephen Covey; **89 Simon Sinek:** Quoted by Simon Sinek; **90, 120, 140 and 190 Maggie Alphonsi:** Quoted by Maggie Alphonsi. Used with permission; **91–92, 95 and 125 Andrew Strauss:** Andrew Strauss – Personal interview with authors 2019. Used with permission; **93 Berrett-Koehler Publishers:** Adapted from Reina, D & Reina, M (2015)

Trust and Betrayal in the Workplace. Building effective relationships in the workplace. EDS publications Ltd.; **107 Tenzin Gyatso:** Quoted by Tenzin Gyatso; **117 Alex Ferguson:** Quoted by Sir Alex Ferguson; **117 Studs Terkel:** Quoted by Studs Terkel; **118–119 Mihaly Csikszentmihalyi:** Quoted by Mihaly Csikszentmihalyi; **119 Steve Jobs:** Quoted by Steve Jobs; **119 Milton Friedmann:** Quoted by Milton Friedmann; **121 Regan Gallo:** Quoted by Regan Gallo; **123 American Psychological Association:** Shalom Shwartz: this is from Schwartz, S. H. and Bilsky, W. (1990). Toward a theory of the universal content and structure of values: Extensions and cross cultural replications. Journal of Personality and Social Psychology, 58, 878–891; **127 Jamie Dimer:** Quoted by Jamie Dimer; **127 NASA:** Statements are the ones developed by the NASA Space Centre in the 1960; **127–128 Kevin Roberts:** Quoted by Kevin Roberts; **129 Bill Gates:** Quoted by Bill Gates; **129 Elon Musk:** Quoted by Elon Musk; **136 Adrian Moorhouse:** Quoted by Adrian Moorhouse; **141 John Wooden:** Quoted by John Wooden; **143 Pearson Education:** Dent, Fiona; Brent, Mike; The Leader's Guide To Influence ePUB eBOOK: How to use Soft Skills to get Hard Results, 1st ED., ©2011. Reprinted by permission of Pearson Education Limited; **150 Hachette Book Group:** Adapted from Whitmore, J (2010) Coaching for Performance: the principles and practise of coaching and leadership. Nicolas Brealey; **161 Heraclitus:** Quoted by Heraclitus; **162 John Wiley & Sons, Inc.:** Bill Joiner and Stephen Josephs, in their excellent book, Leadership Agility 2007; **177 Carl Rogers:** Quoted by Carl Rogers; **185 Harvard Business Publishing:** Pulse Survey – Meeting the Challenges of Developing Collaborative Teams for Future Success: Harvard Business Review Analytic Services.

Image credits:

13 Alima Kassenova: Courtesy of Alima Kassenova; **14 Sam Davies:** Courtesy of Samantha Davies; **15 Neil Loft:** Courtesy of Neil Loft.

CHAPTER 1

INTRODUCTION

INTRODUCTION

Being able to develop and work in effective teams is a critical factor in the success of an organisation. According to a research report by Deloitte University Press (2016) *'Businesses are reinventing themselves as networks of teams in order to keep pace with the challenges of a fluid unpredictable world'*. In this book we have gathered together a number of essential team working skills, attitudes and behaviours that we collectively feel will help you to build, develop and sustain teams that work well in this unpredictable world.

WHERE DOES THE WORD 'TEAM' COME FROM?

The word 'Team' derives from the old English and Norse word for bridle, and from that came the meaning of a set of animals, harnessed together, which would pull ploughs to till the land. From this definition comes the analogy of people involved in joint action. The concept of 'team' must be one of the most commonly used ideas in organisational life. Although we think that it is overused, in the sense that many so-called teams are not in fact real teams but rather a group of people who work together.

WHAT IS A TEAM?

The usual definition of a team is, 'A small group of people with complementary skills and a common purpose'. Small, because too many people will make it ineffective. The accepted range for an effective team tends to be between 5 and 12 people, although Wharton Business School Professor Jennifer Mueller concludes that 6 is optimal. But although important, the number of people is not as important as the quality and skill of the people and the type of leadership demonstrated within the team. Teams need complementary skills, because you need people with different skills and preferences to gain the maximum amount of diversity and common purpose. For the team to achieve anything it needs to have discussed and agreed its common purpose. It's actually quite amazing how many so-called teams there are which have not discussed the issue of complementarity or indeed common purpose.

Researchers Jon Katzenbach and Douglas Smith made the useful distinction between working groups and teams. They are not the same thing and have different goals and objectives, need different skills and produce different results. Working groups, for example, share information, perspectives and insights. They place their focus on individual goals and accountabilities, and not on taking responsibility for results other than their own, whereas teams also focus on mutual accountability and responsibility. There are a number of other differences between working groups and teams. Teams, for example, have a specific team purpose as well as the more general organisation mission to follow. A group is likely to have a specific leader, whereas a real team will also have a leader and the ability to share leadership roles.

The main thing to remember is that just because you call a group of people working together a team, that doesn't magically make them a team. Until you work to develop specific team attributes, it will be a working group. That said, effective working groups can be more productive than ineffective teams. But at their best, real teams will outperform working groups.

As we have mentioned, the world we are living in is an extremely complex one, so it is increasingly difficult for one person (no matter how brilliant and how high up the hierarchy) to have the answer to all the problems and dilemmas our organisations face. However, we do still sometimes face less complex issues: ones which are fairly well known and where there is no uncertainty. These issues can be described as 'puzzles', and they can be solved by individuals. So, when faced by puzzles, we can often act and decide alone. On the other hand, when we face more complexity and less certainty about an issue, we can describe it either as a problem (has potential solutions) or as a dilemma (doesn't actually have any one single solution). When faced with a problem we need to work in teams in order to leverage diversity, get different opinions and challenges and see how we can use the collective intelligence of the team to find the best possible solution. When faced with even greater uncertainty – a dilemma – we still need to use a team, but now we need a high-performing, complex team to help work out the different options and possibilities for action. So, we need divergent thinking, challenge and honesty at this level, and this requires a highly effective and sophisticated team.

Psychologist John Gottman – a specialist in human relationships – believes that choosing a partner is choosing a set of problems (Gottman, 2011). Problems are an integral part of a relationship, and it's the same with teams. There are no teams without problems – it's how you collectively deal with the problems that arise that makes the team effective or ineffective.

We believe that there is significant progress to be made in how teams work effectively, and that team leaders and team members can realise the full potential of effective teamwork. We hope that this book can contribute to this progress.

In this book you will learn how to:

- understand your preferred leadership approach
- understand your own personality and that of your colleagues
- build psychological safety in your team
- create a diverse team and increase inclusion
- work effectively in virtual teams
- influence without formal authority
- increase the levels of engagement in the team
- understand the different kinds of trust and develop a higher level of trust within your team
- leverage conflict effectively
- understand the importance of, and develop a higher level of purpose and meaning in the team
- give effective feedback
- be an effective coach to both individuals and the team
- better understand the psychology of change
- be an effective team facilitator.

We cover the key skills and capabilities for leading and working in contemporary high-performance teams. This book will be equally useful if you read it in the traditional way of start to finish, or if you prefer to dip in and out depending on your own particular needs and interests. The content is composed of a variety of theories, techniques, tips, case studies, reflective questions and practical exercises to help the reader and their teams develop their skills and capabilities. There is also the opportunity to access a self-awareness inventory – Lumina Spark – to help you understand your own preferences when working in a team.

WHO WE ARE AND WHY WE ARE WRITING THIS BOOK

We could have called this book 'Team Performance', but we are more interested in *when* and *how* teams in business and in sport achieve effective performance. Teams have to work well together and implement a number of key practices and behaviours in order to achieve that performance, so in the book we want to focus on what teams need to do and how they need to work together to achieve their best possible performance. We know that there are some basic things that teams often get wrong and some things they could do, but often don't. So our idea was to combine the theories with the actual practice of team performance in order to give you clear ideas of what will help your teamwork and what will hinder your team from working effectively.

As part of this process, we met with a large number of teams and team members across a wide range of business and sporting contexts, including business leaders, team captains, coaches, chefs, surgeons and military leaders, to try and understand how teams work in their world and discover the key drivers that underpin high-performance teams no matter what the context. We met and spoke with team members and team leaders from many different countries and continents, including Europe, the USA, UK, the United Arab Emirates, Egypt, Mali and South Africa, as well as China, Brazil and Argentina.

All three of us are very motivated by how teams work and how they can work better together and become the best possible team. We believe that leadership should be defined in terms of the ability to build and maintain a high-performing team, which is evaluated in terms of the performance of the team.

We have differing backgrounds. Nigel has coached and led teams at the highest level in sport and business. Fiona has led teams in both business and education and, like Mike, is an executive education specialist, who has trained, coached and facilitated managers and leaders for 30 years across all five continents.

Nigel has experience as a team player at the highest level of international rugby. He captained the England Rugby team on his debut in 1984, making him the youngest player to captain England on their debut, and he also represented the Barbarians and the British Lions – the team that selects the best rugby players from the whole of the UK. He has been a player, team captain and team coach: he coached Wasps and Gloucester in the English Premiership and worked as a high-performance consultant with Reading FC. More recently Nigel has gained great experience in leading high-performance teams as an executive, manager and leader, in his roles as CEO of USA Rugby, Director of Professional Rugby and until recently, acting CEO of the English Rugby Football Union.

He now works as an executive coach with a focus on executive/leadership development and team coaching. His professional development during the last five years has included executive coach training and certification, and he is an active member of the International Coaching Federation (ICF).

Nigel is motivated by wanting to share the many years' experience as a practitioner, developing and leading successful teams and the theory that has supported and underpinned his work. For him, effective teams don't just happen – they develop over time and can deliver amazing results if they focus on the right things.

Mike's rugby career is much less illustrious than Nigel's, though he played rugby for many years in France's second division and has represented his region. He is a Professor of Practice and Adjunct Faculty at Hult International Business School and has written extensively on the subject of leadership. He is an accredited coach and has experience of working with thousands of managers and leaders worldwide, from Brazil to Japan, as an executive trainer, facilitator and coach, and has observed really effective leadership behaviours as well as very poor ones when it comes to leading teams.

Fiona is also a Professor of Practice and Adjunct Faculty at Hult International Business School. She also freelances as a coach, facilitator and executive trainer and has worked with managers from around the world. Previously she was a Director of Executive Education at Ashridge Business School, where she led a team of faculty and two of the business streams involved in aspects of executive education. She has developed a range of psychometric instruments including the Ashridge Inventory of Management Skills and the Influencing Style Preference Inventory, which are still used today. Fiona has authored and co-authored a number of books about leadership, teams, management, career development and women in business. Much of her work has involved working with teams and training and coaching team leaders, all of which have helped her to understand what works and doesn't for good team performance.

We met many years ago in Ashridge Business School (now part of Hult International Business School) when working on the English Rugby Football Union's Elite Coaching Development Programme, and we are really pleased to be working together now to ally the concepts and theories of high-performing teams with the actual practice.

CHAPTER 2

LEADING THE TEAM

'You don't have to hold a position in order to be a leader.'

Henry Ford, founder of the Ford Motor Company

INTRODUCTION

What kind of leader are you? How would you define your leadership style?

In this chapter we will look at two common metaphors for leadership and recommend an approach to team leadership that we think is the most relevant one today.

Two metaphors that have been regularly used in team leadership development are the leader as Hero, and Robert Greenleaf's concept of leader as Servant (Greenleaf, 2002). To explain these more fully, the leader as hero is typically the type of boss who knows what he or she wants, has a clear sense of direction, doesn't really want to hear ideas from the team and is not afraid to step forward and tell the team what to do. This seems to be quite a common occurrence in teams. But that of course is the extreme end. At the other end of the spectrum is the Servant Leader metaphor; typically, the servant leader would be the kind of team leader who steps back, asks questions, observes and listens to the team members. They would see themselves as being in service to the team and the organisation.

Reality more often than not lies somewhere along the spectrum and is often messy and confused. Some leaders encourage team members to speak up but then don't really listen or listen politely enough and then ignore or discard the team members' ideas. Or the leader listens and acts on ideas but then, if there are many different ideas coming from the team, how do they decide which to act upon?

Let's explore both of these metaphors in a little more detail.

HERO AND SERVANT LEADERSHIP

The leader as hero is deeply ingrained in society, has proved itself as a stubborn metaphor and may be rather difficult to replace. Although it is now criticised and seen as increasingly irrelevant in a VUCA (volatile, uncertain, complex and ambiguous) world, it is, as Harvard scholar and writer Sharon Daloz Parks says, 'A deep and abiding myth' (Parks, 2005, p. 201). Team members sometimes need to feel they are in safe hands and want a clear sense of direction.

But if you have a heroic leader, where does that leave the members of the team? They might then be considered as victims or passive followers. That cannot work in a complex world where we need team members to be responsible, proactive and creative. A good example of this is in the airline industry. In the 1970s there was a spate of accidents in the USA, where human error was found to be the cause. The key factor in this human error was the relationship between the pilots – that is between the Captain and First Officer. Many experienced pilots and perhaps many who had served in the military were quite autocratic in their behaviour. That meant that they thought they knew best and consequently did not accept any challenges or feedback from their First Officers, or indeed any of the crew. The term used by aircrew is 'cockpit gradient', and this refers to the difference in hierarchy between the Captain, First Officer and indeed the rest of the crew on board. When the gradient is too steep, the First Officer is reluctant to oppose or challenge the Captain, even when he or she is fully aware that the Captain is making a fatal error.

As a response, the American Civil Aviation board brought in the concept of CRM – Crew Resource Management. Stuart Greene, a former Captain with British airline Easy Jet, explains that CRM means that the Captain has to be approachable, accept feedback, involve all the crew and consider different options. For Stuart, this means that as Captain, he is obliged to use all resources at his disposal and not just make an autocratic decision. The mnemonic used is DODAR:

- Diagnose (consider)
- Options
- Decide
- Assign tasks
- Review.

This has become an integral part of how teams work on board aircraft and has reduced human error in the cockpit. Other teams would do well to consider using a similar approach, where the team leader is obliged to involve the team in considering alternative options and also in taking time to review the decisions. Stuart explains that reviewing is a critical part of the process as conditions can change all the time, and the initial decision may have to be changed rather than blindly adhered to.

The idea of leader as Servant was put forward some 40 years ago as a deliberate counter to the flawed hero metaphor. Its main proponent was Robert Greenleaf in his book *Servant Leadership*. Though attractive in many ways, it has its downsides too. Although the concept means that the Leader should be in service to the organisation, employees and stakeholders, the metaphor of leader as servant is not entirely appropriate or relevant to our diverse society and it hasn't really taken hold of the management community's imagination.

Hero	Servant
■ Tend to give advice	■ Good at listening carefully
■ Cut discussions short	■ Tend not to interrupt
■ May act without involving others	■ Always seek others' perspectives
■ Are convinced their ideas are best	■ Acknowledge and include others
■ More action than listening oriented	■ Able to step back
■ Tend to step forward and give direction	■ Seek contributions from others

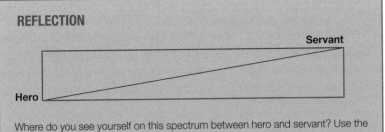

REFLECTION

Where do you see yourself on this spectrum between hero and servant? Use the table above to determine your preference. If you tend towards the leader as hero end, then it's likely that you need to focus on listening more, involving your team members and stepping back more often to give space to others.

If on the other hand you tend towards the leader as servant end, where you are good at listening to others and involving people, then you might need to think about stepping forward more, sharing your thoughts and ideas more clearly and setting clear boundaries.

HOST LEADERSHIP

We believe that Dr Mark McKergow's concept of the leader as 'Host' is a useful way of helping leaders resolve these issues (McKergow, 2009). This metaphor offers a useful rethinking of both hero and servant leadership traditions. By building on both these models it offers an interesting and relevant new way to conceptualise team leadership behaviours in the face of increasing complexity and change.

The act of hosting – receiving or entertaining guests or strangers – is as old as mankind. Hosts sometimes have to act heroically, stepping forward, planning, inviting, introducing, providing. They also act in service – stepping back, encouraging, giving space, joining in. The Host can be seen encompassing aspects of both metaphors and the movement between them.

THE SIX ROLES AND FOUR POSITIONS OF THE HOST LEADER

To summarise the concept of Host Leadership let us offer you the six roles and four positions that the Host Leader can take.

1. Initiator – Getting things started.
2. Inviter – Thinking invitationally. Inviting people and contributions.
3. Space creator – Creating the space for people to speak up and express themselves.
4. Gatekeeper – Including or, where needed, excluding.
5. Connector – Making connections and introductions.
6. Co-participator – Joining in as a contributor and team member.

The six roles
(copyright McKergow & Bailey, used with permission)

You might like to think about which of these roles resonate with you the most and the least. Ideally you will be able to adopt each of these roles depending upon the context of the situation.

The four positions are outlined below.

1. In the *Spotlight*: up front, in full view. Taking the lead.
2. With the *Guests*: participating and contributing with your colleagues.
3. In the *Gallery*: when you need to have an overview. The so-called helicopter perspective.
4. In the *Kitchen*: a private reflective space. A place and time to stand back and reflect on what is going on.

The four positions
(copyright McKergow & Bailey, used with permission)

As a leader you need to be able to adopt all of these four positions and the six roles when required. You will be less effective if you are stuck in just one or two of these positions. If you are always up front and in the spotlight, then you are not shining the light on your team members and giving them enough credit. But if you are always in the kitchen and no one sees you, then that is also unsatisfactory.

IMPLICATIONS OF HOST LEADERSHIP

There are several implications of Host Leadership. A leader as host would be:

- **Relational** – hosting can *only* happen with others (guests). In our example the guests would be the team members.
- **Invitational** – hosts tend to use 'soft power' and a welcoming hand rather than coercion.
- **Creating meaning** – providing a context for new interactions and sense-making to occur.
- **Thinking in phases** – looking *around* the task and including preparation and reflection as integral activities of leadership.
- **Taking care** – the host has a traditional primary role in safeguarding their guests and, in this case, it would mean taking care of the team and their needs.
- **Taking responsibility** – and therefore being accountable for what happens, whether planned or not. This implies that the team leader cannot just blame the team if things go wrong.

STEPPING FORWARDS AND BACK

As a Host Leader you are alternating between stepping forwards (and acting somewhat heroically) and stepping back (serving, providing, leaving space open for others). To do this the Host Leader needs three things.

Awareness – of the spectrum of possibilities and how they connect with the organisation and its work.

Flexibility – to actually act and perform effectively in different places along the hero–servant spectrum.

Timing – the contextual intelligence to know *when* to act, when to move, when to stand back and when to change tack.

When stepping forward you are defining expectations. When stepping forward the team leader would gather people together and set expectations. They would want to help everyone get clear about:

- team goals
- what each person is bringing to the table – skills, knowledge, etc.
- what's important to you about HOW things will proceed – expectations and boundaries.

Here you have stepped forward and set the frame. However, as you want to get the most out of your team, it's important to remember to step back a bit and allow contributions from others.

When stepping back you are creating space for interaction. When stepping back you would be keen to give the team a chance to get involved. This means using *all* the resources at your disposal. This doesn't mean being inactive – on the contrary, you will want to be alert and responsive. You can:

- Ask open questions to draw out people's expertise. Here you could ask questions such as– 'What do *you* think Jane?' or, 'I'd like to hear your perspective on that Fran'. Then be sure to give your team members the space to respond properly.

- Encourage discussion. This means that you signal that you are open to changing things and so you actively involve people and give them time to discuss the ideas on the table. Good discussion means that people allow each other to finish their sentences, build on each other's thoughts, avoid judgemental remarks and avoid the dreaded phrase 'I agree, BUT ...'.

- Model good behaviour by being appreciative of your team members' ideas, building on them and sharing how you intend to use the team's collective thoughts.

When you are actively stepping back there might be a slow start to things, but hang in there. Give your team members a chance. You gathered these people together, and if you want to get the most out of them, you owe them the opportunity to get involved. It can be hard to open up a space for others to interact and it can feel a bit like you are losing control. But you are not losing control. On the contrary, you are still there, listening and engaged. And when the time comes, you can step forward again and nudge things back on track if you feel it's necessary.

When to step back and when to step forward? If you want more involvement, step back a bit more often, and wait to see what happens. If things are getting too far-off track, step forward and check that people are clear about what is expected and that you have a common understanding of what's wanted. You will then develop a sense of how this works in your own team.

A good example of stepping forwards and back is if you are at the beginning of a new project. You might initially step forward to headline the overall goals and intent of the project. Then you would step back and invite questions about the project. You might even encourage any challenges and have an open discussion which would allow the project team members to make suggestions and improvements. After this you might finish the meeting by stepping forward again to summarise what has been agreed, and then step back once more to listen to action plans and commitments from each project team member.

EXAMPLE

Jonathon, an expert, writer and researcher was appointed CEO of a major business school on the strength of his academic knowledge and qualifications. While he was undoubtedly world class in his knowledge, he had little knowledge or expertise in actually leading a team of some 350 people. He was somewhat introverted and ill at ease socially and so tended to keep himself to himself. The result was that the people in the business school felt he was not interested in them and that there was a lack of clear direction. Jonathon remained in the kitchen or in the gallery and did not adopt the 'with the guest' or 'in the spotlight' positions.

Of course, the outcome would have been just as unsatisfactory if he had always assumed the 'in the spotlight' or 'with the guests' positions. The challenge is to be able to adopt all four positions in a flexible way depending on the context.

FINALLY

When you face a leadership challenge, you might like to consider using the ideas in this chapter to decide which, out of all the choices open to you, you want to take. We suggest that you first of all consider whether you need to be stepping back or forwards. After that you can reflect which of the six roles you can take – for example, will you be the Inviter or does the situation demand that you act as Gatekeeper? Then consider which position you need to be in. Will it be stepping back into the Kitchen in order to think deeply about the situation and gain an overall perspective? Or should it be stepping forward in the Spotlight and assuming responsibility. Each and every situation demands a different response and the six roles and four positions of Host Leadership offer a really useful way of navigating the choices every leader has to make.

CHAPTER 3

UNDERSTANDING SELF AND OTHERS

'If you will not reveal yourself to others, you cannot reveal yourself to yourself.'

Jordan B. Petersen, Canadian author and psychologist

The Oracle at Delphi in ancient Greece used to advise those who consulted it to 'Know thyself'. For a team to work effectively it's still essential for the team leader and team members to know themselves well, and for the team members to know the leader and their colleagues really well. One of the best ways to know each other is for the team to undertake a personality profile so that they can share each other's preferences, understand each other better and consequently can interact more effectively. The benefits of this are:

- understanding each other's strengths and blind spots
- having a clear structure on which to base a discussion
- having a common language to review each other's preferences and the implications for working together.

But does a team member's personality influence teamwork? Psychologist and author Robert Hogan states that personality is a stable predictor of team performance, so it is useful to explore team members' different personalities to see how they can work effectively together (Hogan, 2017).

EFFECTIVE TEAMS DEPEND ON GOOD TEAM PLAYERS

We know from the research that teams with certain profiles do better or worse in terms of performance. So, if you are interested in high team performance it makes sense to undertake a well-researched personality profile among team members. Apart from cognitive ability, the personality variables that affect team performance are the so-called Big Five personality factors, and each one of these is measured on a scale of high to low. The bullet list below explains each of the variables.

- Openness – High = inventive and curious. Low = consistent and cautious.
- Conscientiousness – High = efficient and organised. Low = extravagant and careless.
- Extraversion – High = outgoing and energetic. Low = solitary and reserved.
- Agreeableness – High = Friendly and compassionate. Low = Critical and rational.
- Emotional stability or Neuroticism – High = Sensitive and nervous. Low = Resilient and confident.

These are the Big Five personality factors and many large organisations will use a variation of these to assess their people during training or as part of their performance management processes. Not all team members are good team players. We have seen countless teams whose work has been disrupted by poor team players. One example we see a lot is people with high technical skills but who are disagreeable or emotionally unstable. No matter how good they are technically, they always seem to disrupt the team, upsetting others and generally being unable to get on with others.

So our recommendation would be – if at all possible – to look at each team member's preferences and then discuss how these show up within the team context, relationships and tasks. It stands to reason that if you have team members who lack, for example, conscientiousness, and the tasks require a measure of this attribute, then it will not perform effectively. On the other hand, a team of people with high conscientiousness may be lacking in its opposite, which is adaptability and flexibility: in that scenario the team would not achieve optimal performance.

It is hard to give feedback to a colleague based on the classic Big Five characteristics. For instance, you may have to tell someone that on their assessment they rated as low Openness, low Conscientiousness, and are Introverted, Disagreeable and Neurotic or emotionally unstable! Typically debriefing on the Big Five demands a skilled psychologist to ensure the correct process and full understanding.

However, there are other tools that are more user friendly; one that we find particularly useful was developed by researcher Dr Stewart Desson. He created the Lumina Spark assessment in which:

- Openness is framed as a continuum between – Big Picture or Down to Earth.
- Conscientiousness between – Inspiration Driven or Disciplined.
- Extraversion and Introversion remain the same.
- Agreeableness becomes – People or Outcome focused.
- Neuroticism – or emotional stability – is not measured in this particular instrument.

The idea is that the team members can assess their preferences, reflect on what that means for them as colleagues and gain a better understanding of their colleagues' preferences so as to work more effectively together. Lumina Spark also makes it possible to look at the total composition of the team in order to see how balanced it is overall and to understand some of the dynamics at play between different team members.

Another aspect that comes into play in team performance is the concept of **overdone strengths**. A team member's key strengths can easily become weaknesses when overdone. This happens especially when someone is stressed. Confidence, for example, which is an important trait for high-potential managers, can become over-confidence and arrogance. A preference for achieving results can become bullying. High agreeableness can become over-pleasing. So, it is important that you recognise not only your own and your team's strengths but also your and your team's potential overdone strengths. This will enable you to help each other mitigate these overdone strengths before they become a problem. When someone is in the zone of overdone strengths then they are negatively affecting both relationships and performance in the team.

TOOLS THAT HELP WITH SELF- AND OTHERS' AWARENESS

Of course, there are many tools that can be used to improve self-awareness in the team. Among the many that we have used are Myers Briggs Type Index (MBTI), Fundamental Interpersonal Relationship Orientation (FIRO), Strengths Deployment Inventory (SDI), Team Management Systems (TMS), Belbin and Hogan profiles. They are all extremely useful as a catalyst for discovery, reflection and sharing preferences and their implications.

We, however, would like to focus on two specific tools that we feel are extremely helpful in the team environment. One is Spotlight, created by Mindflick, a consultancy co-founded by former England Cricket captain, Sir Andrew Strauss; the other is the Lumina Spark psychometric questionnaire created by Dr Stewart Desson, which we mentioned earlier in the chapter.

Let's look first of all at Spotlight. The goal of the tool is to help individuals broaden their perception of their personality, to give them more flexibility when finding solutions to thrive at work and in life (e.g. working with others, performing under pressure). Conceptually, Spotlight is operationalised as two distinct models that relate to individuals' *behavioural style* preferences: (a) the FLEX model, and their *mindset* preferences in situations where there is perceived to be something to win or lose; and (b) the COPE model.

The FLEX model was developed based on two of the 'Big Five' personality traits which we discussed above – namely 'Extraversion' and 'Agreeableness'. By combining characteristics associated with each end of the scale of these two traits (ensuring that each characteristic was positively framed), four distinct behavioural style preferences were generated that make up the FLEX model:

- forceful (external Task Focused)
- logical (internal Task Focused)
- empathetic (internal People Focused)
- expressive – written as eXpressive (external People Focused).

Each of these four styles is associated with a set of personal characteristics that describe an individual's *behavioural* preferences:

- **Forceful** – this is where team members are action oriented, take control, are fast paced and direct.
- **Logical** – team members with this preference tend to be analytical, detailed and precise.
- **Empathetic** – team members with this preference tend to be reflective, encouraging, care for fellow team members and are values driven.
- **Expressive** – team members with this preference like to connect with others, are enthusiastic, interactive and tend to be persuasive.

The COPE model was developed based on Jeffrey Gray's 'Reinforcement Sensitivity Theory', which looks at individual differences in the sensitivity of basic brain systems that respond to punishing and reinforcing stimuli, thought to underlie certain personality dimensions (Gray, 1970). The personality characteristics that are associated with two central factors of this theory, which measure Reward Sensitivity (RS) and Punishment Sensitivity (PS), were used to generate four distinct *mindset* preferences that make up the COPE model:

- contained (low PS and low RS)
- optimistic (low PS and high RS)
- prudent (high PS and low RS)
- engaged (high PS and high RS).

Like the FLEX model, each of these four mindsets is associated with a set of personal characteristics that describe an individual's preferences when it is perceived that something can be won or lost (i.e., Reward and Punishment). The COPE model will give you an indication of your sensitivity to reward or your sensitivity to threat.

- **Contained** – people with this preference, i.e. low sensitivity to both Punishment and Reward, tend to stick with their decisions, making the assumption that it is the right course of action.

- **Optimistic** – people with this preference, i.e. low sensitivity to Punishment and high sensitivity to Reward, tend to want to just go ahead and get things done.

- **Prudent** – people with this preference, i.e. high sensitivity to Punishment and low sensitivity to Reward, tend to see the danger in a given situation and want to proceed cautiously.

- **Engaged** – people with this preference, i.e. high sensitivity to both Punishment and Reward, tend to want to stay highly alert as their mindset is that things could change quickly.

The Spotlight report gives you, among others, an indication of factors such as:

- your preferences on the FLEX and COPE models described above
- your drivers
- your strengths, overdone strengths and blind spots
- what gives you confidence
- your resilience and energy
- what your main stressors are
- how you react under pressure.

Nigel has used Spotlight extensively and has found that it focusses on an area of team development that he had always found fascinating as a team leader. He had been aware of how people can start to behave differently when the context changed, and Spotlight helped him to understand that shift in behaviour and use it to his advantage. When the context changes, when there is something to be won or lost, when the pressure comes on, or when there is a deadline to hit, you start to see individual, team behaviour and mindset change. If you understand how your team will react to these changes, you can lead your team more effectively and improve results.

In a recent interview with Forbes magazine, Andrew Strauss said:

It's about understanding that different contexts are going to ask different things of you. Especially when you are under pressure, our default is to become more fixed and rigid, and that's where the really big mistakes happen. On the sporting field, in a business environment, in an exam situation, rigidity and being fixed is unhealthy. To try and understand ways of staying adaptable under pressure is crucial. The world is dynamic, it is always shifting and changing, and you need to be able to shift and change with it, especially when you are under pressure.

So Spotlight can help identify useful behaviours and help team members understand how they react to pressure. For more information about this specific tool go to https://spotlightprofile.com and navigate to 'Spotlight' under the Products tab.

THE LUMINA SPARK PSYCHOMETRIC

Let's look now in more detail at the Lumina Spark psychometric, which Mike and Fiona have used extensively when working with teams, and which is an extremely powerful tool to help develop effective teams. In the model below we see the 8 characteristics and 24 qualities that are measured by the Lumina Spark tool. Each characteristic has three qualities.

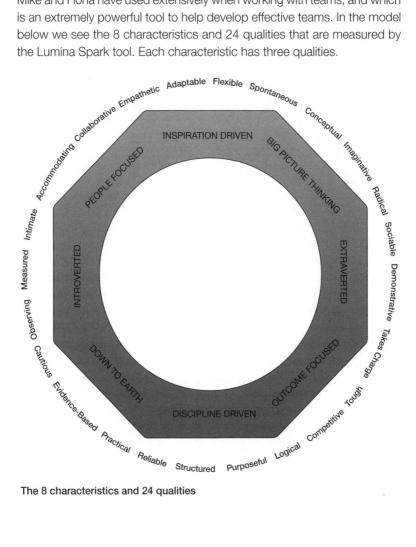

The 8 characteristics and 24 qualities

So, for example the characteristic of People Focused has the three qualities of:

- accommodating
- collaborative
- empathetic.

while the characteristic of its opposite – Outcome Focused – has the three qualities of:

- tough
- competitive
- logical.

This model can be used with or without filling in the questionnaire. You could use it by asking the team members to identify three key strengths or preferences that they have, and to give an example of how they apply when they are at their best. This would then help team members to know each other's strengths and preferences and enable them to work more effectively together. For example, if Harmy indicates that he is accommodating, collaborative and empathetic and his colleague Ama indicates that she is tough, competitive and logical, then they can discuss how best to accommodate each other's preferences and how these strengths complement each other within the team. Without this awareness and sharing of strengths and preferences the danger is that Ama thinks that Harmy is not competitive enough and Harmy feels that Ama is not collaborative enough, and this can quickly lead to conflict.

Another exercise you can do with the team is to then ask team members to think about their overdone strengths. When they are tired, frustrated or stressed how might their strengths turn into weaknesses? To illustrate this, look at the model on the next page which details the overdone strengths. For example, when stressed, someone who has a preference for being evidence based and who pays attention to details might become overly attentive to getting the facts right and become lost in the details. We are all capable of overplaying our strengths in some circumstances, and by acknowledging this and sharing these, we become more able to understand and support each other in the team.

OVERDONE STRENGTHS

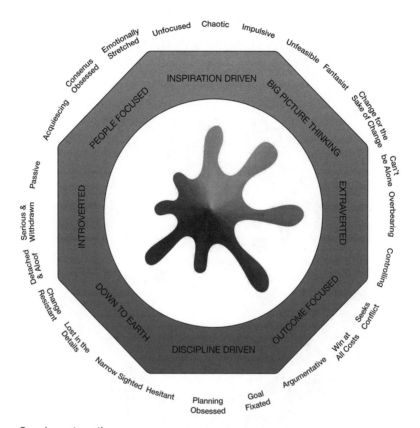

Overdone strengths

You can see from the model above that the strengths of being competitive and tough can, when overdone, flip over into winning at all costs and seeking conflict. A recognition of what causes us to flip into overdone strengths and having open conversations in the team about what we can do about it will lead to less disengagement and higher performance.

Having done these simple exercises, you will be able to paint a picture of the team's overall strengths and its overdone strengths. This will allow you to recognise whether you need to bring in specific people with specific strengths in areas where the team is lacking. For example, a Research and Development team might have great strengths in both detail and in big picture thinking but be lacking communication skills towards the external environment. Or a Technology team with strong preferences in detail and results focus might be lacking in people and big picture skills. If this is not recognised and dealt with the team will not perform to its potential.

The interesting thing about Lumina is that it looks at three different aspects of each quality. So it distinguishes between your underlying preference, the way you show up at work and also when you overdo a particular preference (the overextended persona).

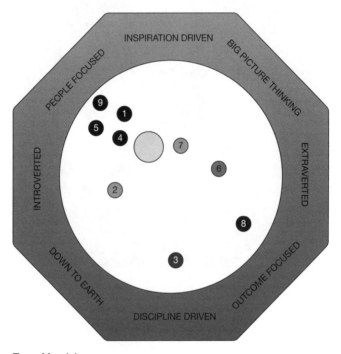

Team Mandala

The Team Mandala is a composite summary showing the overall strengths and preferences of the team. So at a glance all the team members can visualise the team's preferences and then have a discussion about what the implications might be. The team in the model above has an overall preference for being People Focused. This is absolutely fine but the question that might be asked is, 'Is there enough focus on outcomes and results?' And what is the relationship like between the people who are People Focused and the one person who is Outcome Focused? The idea is not that any one profile is right or wrong, but it enables the team to have an open and honest conversation about strengths and overdone strengths and any gaps.

The 24 Qualities that make up your Everyday Persona

The percentages indicate where you score in relation to the general working population.
For example a score of over 50% would put you in the top half of the population.

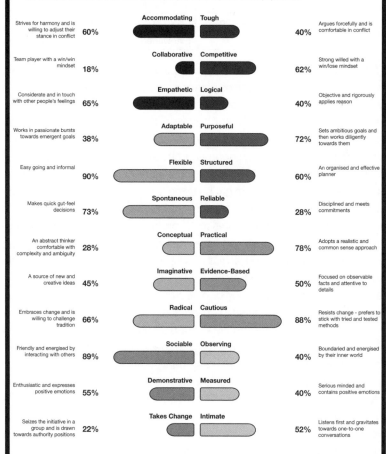

Left description	Score	Accommodating	Tough	Score	Right description
Strives for harmony and is willing to adjust their stance in conflict	60%	Accommodating	Tough	40%	Argues forcefully and is comfortable in conflict
Team player with a win/win mindset	18%	Collaborative	Competitive	62%	Strong willed with a win/lose mindset
Considerate and in touch with other people's feelings	65%	Empathetic	Logical	40%	Objective and rigorously applies reason
Works in passionate bursts towards emergent goals	38%	Adaptable	Purposeful	72%	Sets ambitious goals and then works diligently towards them
Easy going and informal	90%	Flexible	Structured	60%	An organised and effective planner
Makes quick gut-feel decisions	73%	Spontaneous	Reliable	28%	Disciplined and meets commitments
An abstract thinker comfortable with complexity and ambiguity	28%	Conceptual	Practical	78%	Adopts a realistic and common sense approach
A source of new and creative ideas	45%	Imaginative	Evidence-Based	50%	Focused on observable facts and attentive to details
Embraces change and is willing to challenge tradition	66%	Radical	Cautious	88%	Resists change - prefers to stick with tried and tested methods
Friendly and energised by interacting with others	89%	Sociable	Observing	40%	Boundaried and energised by their inner world
Enthusiastic and expresses positive emotions	55%	Demonstrative	Measured	40%	Serious minded and contains positive emotions
Seizes the initiative in a group and is drawn towards authority positions	22%	Takes Change	Intimate	52%	Listens first and gravitates towards one-to-one conversations

In the chart above we see the 24 qualities of a person's everyday preferences. These are based on the eight aspects:

Inspiration driven	Discipline driven
People focus	Outcome focus
Big picture thinking	Down to earth thinking
Introverted	Extraverted

What is particularly helpful is that, unlike some other psychometric tools, the Lumina Spark tool embraces paradox – it embodies seemingly opposite personality traits at the same time. For example, we can be both extraverted and introverted in different contexts. If you have filled in the Lumina questionnaire each team member will be able to see these 24 qualities in underlying mode, everyday mode and overextended mode. This enables each team member to raise their awareness of their underlying strengths and preferences, how they might be using them at work in everyday mode (or not using them) and when these might be overdone. So in the example above the team member expresses a preference for being logical AND empathetic. In other cases, we have seen team members express a high preference for logical and a really low preference for empathetic. This doesn't mean they are not nice people – but it tends to mean that their responses are focused on logic, on solving the problem, rather than on listening and allowing others to express their emotions.

We see real issues being played out because of these differences and we feel it is essential for teams to have these open and honest conversations about the differences. These conversations can happen with or without taking a particular psychometric questionnaire. You could use the information on the chart above – The 24 qualities – as a catalyst and structure for these conversations. So you could take each of the qualities and work through the list expressing your own preferences and then discussing the implications with your team colleagues.

For instance, if you take the first qualities of Intimate and Takes Charge, you could find that many of your colleagues, like yourself, are tending towards Taking Charge, which means that they are assertive, enjoy influencing and like to take the lead. Perhaps only a few express a preference for Intimate, which means they like to listen, they are low key and prefer one-on-one conversations. A profile like this could mean too much competitiveness, a lack of listening in the team and possibly a complete overwhelming of those people who have a preference for being Intimate. This is one example of the behavioural challenges that can be identified through the use of a structured process to understand self and others.

Over time you may like to work through each of the 24 qualities with your team to gain a higher level of awareness and understanding of each other's preferences, and consequently this can lead to improved team performance.

YOUR PROFILE

The lovely people at Lumina Learning have offered our readers the opportunity to obtain their own Lumina Spark Portrait. So, you can download the link below to complete a questionnaire to obtain a free mini-portrait containing your personal Splash. Your Splash will identify your preferences on the eight Aspects shown in the figure below.

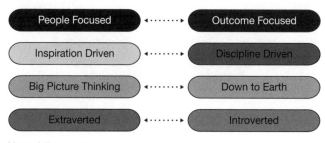

Your eight aspects

And it will look like the figure below – but will be in colour in your personal report!

The colours in your report will correspond to the eight Aspects and the length of each dimension reflects the strength of each Aspect in your portrait. Your Spark Portrait will enable you to increase your own self-awareness and of course you will be able to share it with your colleagues. Based on this portrait, you could ask for feedback about how your preferences affect them and the team overall. To obtain your personal Lumina Spark Portrait, simply go to the following link: https://lumina.xyz/TeamsThatWork

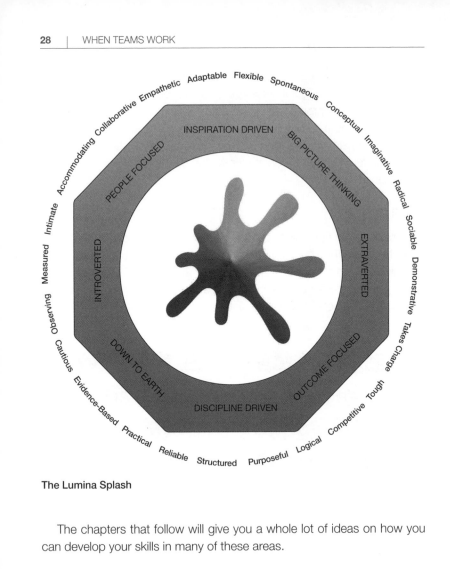

The Lumina Splash

The chapters that follow will give you a whole lot of ideas on how you can develop your skills in many of these areas.

CHAPTER 4

BUILDING PSYCHOLOGICAL SAFETY

'Psychological safety isn't about being nice. It's about giving candid feedback, openly admitting mistakes and learning from each other.'

Dr Amy Edmondson

INTRODUCTION

In this chapter we will examine the concept of psychological safety, look at why it is an important concept for effective teams and give you ideas on how to build effective psychological safety within your team. Research shows that a high level of psychological safety within an organisation leads to much more effective teamwork and better results. This is especially so when the team is facing highly complex issues where there is no certainty and where there is a high need for interdependence. A high level of psychological safety leads to increased performance.

ORIGINS OF PSYCHOLOGICAL SAFETY

The construct of psychological safety has its roots in research on organisational change, in which MIT Professors Edgar Schein and Warren Bennis discussed the need to create psychological safety for individuals if they are to feel secure and capable of changing (Bennis, 2009; Schein, 1996). In 1990, Boston University's William Kahn was able to show how psychological safety can nurture employee engagement. He looked at how people at work could engage and express themselves as opposed to disengaging and being defensive at work. Clearly, engaged team members will perform more effectively than disengaged ones, so a high degree of psychological safety will be important for you to have in your team, if you are aiming for a team that works well.

WHAT EXACTLY IS PSYCHOLOGICAL SAFETY?

Professor Amy Edmondson of Harvard Business School defines psychological safety as a belief that one will not be punished or humiliated for speaking up with ideas, questions, concerns or for making mistakes. And David Burkus, Associate Professor of Leadership and Innovation at Oral Roberts University in Tulsa, USA, defines it as 'the measure of how free people on a team feel to share their ideas, their experiences and their whole selves with each other' (Burkus, 2021).

Both these definitions highlight the importance of having a work environment which is safe for interpersonal risk taking. That means feeling able to speak up with your ideas, thoughts, suggestions and questions. Feeling safe means that you will not be blamed, judged or ridiculed for speaking up, and that you have the confidence to voice any concerns you have without fear.

However, in our opinion it is quite rare to see a really high level of psychological safety in teams, or indeed in many working environments. We believe that not only is it challenging to create and maintain an environment of psychological safety, but there is also a range of barriers to overcome if it is to be achieved.

At this point you may like to reflect and assess how psychologically safe your team or environment is. Start by considering the following areas then score and make notes about your initial thoughts. Score 1 if your response is low and 5 if it is high. You should be scoring at least 3 on each question. Ideally your average will be 4 or 5. If the scores are less than 3 then this is an area that needs to be addressed by asking the team for suggestions on what practical measures can be taken. You then need to agree on specific behaviours and on how team members are held accountable for actions and behaviours. If your average is 3 then this is still an area for improvement. Look at what can be improved so that psychological safety is optimal within your team.

REFLECTION

Assessment of Psychological Safety in my Team		
	Score 1 to 5	Notes
How comfortable are team members to ask questions, challenge and raise difficult issues?		
How well do I know my fellow team members?		
Are mistakes tolerated and learned from?		
Do all team members contribute in an even way?		
Is feedback between members part of the team culture?		
Is debate encouraged?		

WHY PSYCHOLOGICAL SAFETY IS IMPORTANT FOR TEAMS?

High psychological safety requires a supportive organisational culture, *plus* a highly effective team leader *plus* all team members being fully and genuinely aware and supportive of the concept. To achieve this requires determination, skill and honesty. We have seen, and heard, many team leaders and members proudly voice their pride at having high psychological safety in their team, yet when we have interviewed the team members individually, they have told us a different story. Achieving high levels of psychological safety requires a great deal of skill; for example, you need to be aware of the effect you can have on others by simply shaking your head or rolling your eyes at someone's suggestion. Although these actions might not be done consciously or deliberately, they might be viewed by team members as disinterest or disagreement.

It is also important to pay attention to your team members' body language in order to notice when they want to come in and say something, and on top of that have the ability to invite them to come in and contribute, and then restrain yourself from being over critical or dismissive.

But even when management insists that there is a high level of psychological safety, and where team members are actually invited to speak up, many of them will be thinking, 'If I say what I really think, is this going to be a career-limiting challenge?' And if we are not 100 per cent sure that it is safe, then we shut up and take our moans and complaints to our trusted colleagues over a coffee. The boss then never hears what we have to say, and the issue is once again swept under the carpet.

For us there are different levels of psychological safety. We have seen teams where there is a high level, others where there is what we would call a neutral level and still others where psychological safety was very low. The model below illustrates one way of examining and explaining levels of psychological safety in your team or environment.

It can be revealing to examine the level of psychological safety that exists in your team or teams (we show you how to do this later in the chapter) and even more useful if you link the level of Psychologica safety with the amount of pressure there is to be accountable and responsible. There are four major options:

Low Psychological safety and Low Responsibility/Accountability

High Psychological safety and Low Responsibility/Accountability

High Responsibility/Accountability and Low Psychological safety

High Responsibility/Accountability and High Psychological safety

1. When both responsibility/accountability and psychological safety levels are low, the result is complacency and low energy. What is needed here is to increase the levels of Psychological safety (by using some of the tips on page 36 for example) and increase performance standards and accountability in the team.

2. If on the other hand you have a high degree of Psychological safety but a low degree of responsibility taking, then the team is likely to be too comfortable. Team members are happy to speak up without fear, but performance standards are low and there is little accountability. The team may be happy, but they are not performing. What is needed is to bring in much needed clear standards of performance and to make sure that team members are held accountable for their actions.

3. We have seen many teams – both in business and in sport – in this situation. Here you have a team where there are strict performance standards, a clear focus on results and a high degree of accountability. But there is no, or little, opportunity for team members to speak up if they are feeling unsure of something or they are overstressed. Paradoxically the over emphasis on results often leads to sub-optimal performance. The obvious antidote here is to increase the feeling of Psychological safety in the team. This needs to be driven by the team leader who must set an example – by listening more, interrupting and judging less, and generally by allowing team members to speak up and voice any concerns.

4. This is the ideal scenario – where the team has a high degree of psychological safety and a high degree of responsibility taking and accountability. This leads to more openness, more honesty about any issues and leads, we believe, to a more sustainably productive team. The challenge here is to ensure that both these parameters remain high and that the team doesn't become complacent.

As we write this, the world is slowly recovering from the grip of the Covid 19 pandemic, the biggest crisis to hit many countries for a generation. It was painfully obvious that in this extremely difficult and complex situation, no one knew exactly what to do. But the teams on the front line – for example in our hospitals – needed everyone to be able to come up with ideas and suggestions, and for leaders to be open minded and admit that they are fallible. According to the doctors we spoke to, this was exactly what happened – with hierarchy becoming less important.

A colonel in the French Gendarmerie told us that they wanted to keep some of the new more open ways of working that have been necessitated by the pandemic. A doctor working on the front line in a London hospital told us that the notions of hierarchy and power had radically changed, and that everyone was being encouraged to offer ideas and suggestions. This led to decisions being made speedily and an acceptance that they wouldn't get everything right first time, but it was necessary to act quickly. The blame culture had been shelved – at least for the time being!

Google carried out extensive research (the so-called 'Aristotle' project) into what made effective teams and one of the factors which turned out to make a real difference was the presence of psychological safety. Remember that Google is a company of some 135,000 people with revenues of around $160 billion in 2018 (source – Statista) and is one of the largest companies in the world. The Google research found that in the most effective teams, members spoke in roughly the same proportion. So long as everyone got a chance to talk, the team did well, but if only one person or a small group spoke all the time, the collective intelligence declined. They also found that the best teams had something called high 'average social sensitivity; in other words team members were skilled at intuiting how others felt based on their tone of voice, their expressions and other nonverbal cues.

Team members have to be able to contribute their thoughts without fear of ridicule and be sure that they will at least be listened to. And teams need to have leaders and team members who can pick up on the body language and the paralinguistics of the team members and notice, for example, when they want to contribute or when they seem to disagree with the point being made.

CASE STUDY

Jane is a newly promoted leader who has a track record of success and high performance as an individual contributor. Although she is an excellent performer, she has no experience of leading others and has not received any training. She is bright, sociable, intelligent, detail-conscious and hard working. All recipes for success? Unfortunately, not, because Jane has not fully understood that to be a leader of people, you have to empathise, listen and trust the team.

An example of this was in the difficult times caused by the Covid 19 pandemic when her team had to work from home. The team had arranged a check-in call at 8 am every morning before getting down to the day's work. An excellent idea in principle. Naturally the team members were expecting just that – a check-in call where everyone gets to check in. Typically, the effective leader went round each team member in turn and asked them what was going on in their world, how they were feeling and gave them a chance to express themselves. But Jane – no doubt from a good intent – told the team what she'd been up to and then spoke for 25 minutes of the 30 minutes allotted time, telling people what they had to do and how to do it.

The result was that the team didn't a chance to express their feelings of anxiety or express their problems and have the opportunity to get help. They ended up frustrated and dissatisfied and much less engaged. So this team was lacking psychological safety, not so much because of Jane's ego or lack of concern, but from a lack of experience of what real leadership is.

We hear stories similar to this one on a regular basis.

BUILDING PSYCHOLOGICAL SAFETY IN YOUR TEAM

There are a variety of different ways to contribute to the creation and development of psychological safety in your team. We highlight six key areas that teams, their leaders and members can develop and model to progress a culture of psychological safety.

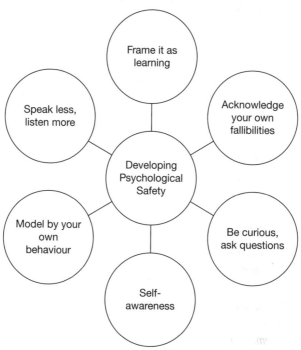

Frame what you are doing as a learning issue and not just an execution issue. This means that it's not just about telling people what to do and how to do it, but focusing on involving everyone who is present, accepting new ideas and thoughts and showing humility as a leader. You may have to accept that the discussion takes a bit longer and that it's a bit messier in order to make sure that everyone is able to contribute. You may be the boss, but you don't necessarily have a monopoly on good ideas. When there is a tremendous level of uncertainty in the world such as during the Covid crisis, you need **all** the brains and voices in the room.

Acknowledge your own **fallibility** as a leader. The Covid 19 pandemic for example is no time for overinflated egos or arrogance. Any leader needs to set the example by demonstrating that they don't know everything. For instance, saying things like 'I may have missed something here' or 'What other ideas do we have?' demonstrates that you recognise that you don't have all the answers and also will encourage others to speak up. Of course, it is also important that any ideas are explored and acted upon.

Be curious, ask questions rather than just making statements and pronouncements. Too often leaders feel that they have to prove their usefulness by telling others what to do, or by making suggestions. To ensure a high level of psychological safety it is more important to listen carefully and ask good questions.

Be self-aware and take a good long look at yourself as a leader or team member. Are you as good as you think you are? Do you know how others see you? How do you get feedback on a regular basis as to how you are actually doing as a leader or how you are performing? If you don't get regular feedback, then we suggest that you find a way to remedy that. If you are afraid of getting feedback, then that suggests that you won't like what you hear. One way of getting regular feedback is to encourage everyone in the team to reflect and share what they think each person is doing well and what they could do differently to be more effective. Get into the habit of incorporating this type of feedback/process into meetings. We have more detail on feedback in Chapter 12.

Model psychological safety. In other words make sure you personally do everything you can to be emotionally aware, to pick up on the non-verbal cues from team members, encourage others to speak up, be appreciative of their contributions and crack down on anyone in the team who interrupts or is dismissive.

Speak less and start listening more! American author Steven Covey said, 'Seek first to understand, then to be understood' (Covey, 2004). He meant that before evaluating, criticising or judging you need to start by listening, asking good questions and trying to understand. Then and only then, do you have the right to give your opinion.

We believe that truly effective teams are those which have a high degree of psychological safety and regularly scan and measure how safe people feel to speak up, challenge and debate.

BARRIERS TO ACHIEVING PSYCHOLOGICAL SAFETY

We mentioned earlier that there are lots of barriers to achieving high psychological safety. These are the implicit, unwritten rules on how people should behave in the team.

Team members commonly hold beliefs like:

- We shouldn't criticise something if it's the boss's idea or if he/she has helped create it.
- We can't speak up unless we have solid evidence and data to back it up.
- It's not a good idea to challenge the boss if the boss is actually present in the room.
- We can't be negative in a group setting if the boss is present.
- Speaking up and challenging will have negative consequences for our careers.

All these implicit rules just serve to prevent psychological safety. If you are the team leader you need to work with your team to specifically address and ensure that these implicit rules are surfaced and then dealt with. You then need to specifically ask to be challenged and welcome, and indeed reward, any challenges. Otherwise, people will not dare to speak up and voice their true opinions. Too often we hear leaders speaking about psychological safety but not actually ensuring that it exists in their team or organisation.

There are two more areas that are worthy of consideration in relation to psychological safety – creativity and innovation and driving out fear.

Creativity and innovation. It is interesting that Professor Edmondson's research shows that people don't just hold back on criticism or challenge if they feel unsafe, but also hold back on bringing new and innovative ideas to the table (Edmondson, 2020). So if we do not have a strong sense of psychological safety, there is a tendency to play it safe, not speak up and not take any risks. This leads to less creativity and innovation which in turn leads to poor results, often at a time when creativity and innovation are essential.

Driving out Fear. One of the key aspects of a team with high psychological safety is the absence of fear. The quality guru W. Edward Deming made eliminating fear one of his key criteria for achieving quality in any process (Deming, 2013). The simple truth is that if people are afraid for any reason they will not speak up and then any quality issues will not be raised, and therefore not resolved.

Michelin-starred Chef Tom Kerridge is clear that fear is a blocker to creativity, engagement and performance.

We allow people to make mistakes, that's the biggest thing, we don't have a fear factor. I am more disappointed in them if they don't have a go at stuff and get it wrong rather than never coming up with an idea. That's really disappointing. Those people don't progress, the ones that do say, 'I have an idea,' or they go ahead and do something, and you end up saying, 'hell what did they do that for?' But you also think that's amazing, they have felt confident enough to do something and use their initiative and that's exciting for us. As a company that's amazing, we are a company that allows people to make mistakes up to a point. (Personal interview with authors, 2021)

Tom's environment is a really demanding and tough one where clients expect the very best. So if he is prepared to allow mistakes in order to nurture growth and creativity, what's stopping you?

Another aspect is that fear prevents learning. In today's extremely complex world, learning is absolutely critical to high performance. The late Reg Revans – the founder of Action Learning – came up with a useful formula about learning. That formula is **L ≥ C**. This means that learning must be equal to or greater than the rate of change in the environment. So if your team's environment is changing quickly, which it probably is, then you and your team need to be prepared to learn even more.

In one US organisation, Bridgewater Associates, no one has the right to hold a critical opinion without speaking up about it. It's absolutely OK to have a negative reaction to something within the organisation, but the founder, Ray Dalio, insists that if you don't agree then you must speak up. This serves to compensate for what usually happens when we disagree with something in the organisation: we moan about it to our trusted colleagues next to the water cooler or over coffee, but when the boss asks us what we think of the latest corporate target or set of priorities, we just say, 'really good' or 'I'm on board', but our heart isn't in it.

MEASURING PSYCHOLOGICAL SAFETY IN YOUR TEAM

Ensuring that a culture of psychological safety is maintained in your team requires regular review. Having an open feedback culture where everyone feels able to give and be willing to receive feedback is a good starting point.

One way of measuring it is to regularly explore a range of areas like those listed below. There should be a low level of:

- degree of interruptions
- levels of judgement and criticism
- speaking behind people's backs
- gossip in general.

And a high level of:

- support and encouragement
- attention paid to body language – yours and others
- tolerance of mistakes
- appreciation shown
- willingness to discuss and debate difficult issues
- confidentiality.

The list above (together with any other areas you wish to explore) can be used as an agenda for a review of how psychologically safe your team is. Building in a regular review either as a meeting in its own right, or taking time at the end of meetings to explore some or all of these issues will help build openness, a culture of feedback and ultimately a psychologically safe environment. One way of starting such a meeting might be to ask each team member to rank the level of psychological safety that they feel exists in the team – use a scale of 1 for low and 10 for high. We find that initially this is best done using Post-it notes. Each person notes down their response and then puts the Post-it onto the wall so that the range of results can be seen by all. It also affords a degree of anonymity which can be lessened as levels of openness and confidence are developed in the team.

You then discuss the numbers and decide together whether they are good enough. If they are. then you speak collectively about how this can be sustained and possibly even improved. If they are not, then the conversation will be about what actions and behaviours will improve the scores.

Finally, we'd like to share a story from Nigel's world of rugby. It illustrates how easy it is for certain behaviours to become part of the norm of any team or group of people. This leads to the creation of accepted rules and customs that are incorporated into the day-to-day culture that subsequently contributes to the levels of psychological safety, high or low, which exist within a team.

CASE STUDY

Previously in rugby, teams were very hierarchical; there was always a group of senior players who would set the standards. For many of these senior players, younger players were a threat to their position in the team, and they would try to suppress rather than encourage their development. Younger players would never be asked to join a team's leadership group (if indeed there was one) and that would have an impact on their future behaviour when they became the senior playing group.

As a young player, you had to be careful where you changed, make sure you followed the rules, worked hard, kept your head down (not up). In some teams, where you sat on the bus travelling to a game would be determined by your age and experience – only the senior players were allowed to sit at the back!

As a young player moving into a successful team, it was a very difficult transition. Firstly, you were selected to replace someone. I remember being selected for my first Yorkshire cap aged 18, replacing a very popular and successful member of the Yorkshire team, who was then moved to the replacements bench. This created a really uncomfortable and pressured situation within the team between some of the more established players and the new arrivals. Secondly, you wanted to perform well and justify your selection, but the environment can create its own pressure and literally put you off your game. It was as if you had to make your way through a maze of psychological challenges to gain the respect and be accepted by the team.

On the other hand, in 1979 I was also selected on the bench for the North of England team that beat the All Blacks in my hometown of Otley. The whole team was stacked with famous international players. They were coached by the great Des Seabrook, a teacher and well-respected coach. I was 18 – talk about walking into a lion's den!

But this environment was very different. Des Seabrook had only a short time to prepare the team, but he made a massive effort to keep me involved. Our captain, Sir Bill Beaumont who was also the England Captain at the time, made time to speak to me and make me feel at home and we remain friends today. Steve Smith, the man I was understudying, became a friend and mentor. This was a very different team, a very different environment and they pulled off one of the biggest shock defeats in world rugby that weekend by beating the world-renowned All Blacks. I remember my excitement and pride riding on the bus to the game, thinking to myself, this team will beat the All Blacks – today nothing will stop them. I learnt a lot about the importance of the team environment that week; it was something that shaped me as a captain, coach and leader.

WHAT LESSONS CAN WE TAKE FROM THIS CASE STUDY?

The environment that exists around the team – the culture of the organisation – is extremely important to the growth and development of any team. Ask yourself how many teams fail to maximise the potential of their individual members because the leader does not take the time to create a psychologically safe environment where everyone feels they can contribute to the success of the team. Creating a psychologically safe environment requires, time, patience, good questions and effective listening skills.

In sports teams it is important to have a psychologically safe environment, especially when it comes to analysing performance. It can be very uncomfortable for a player who has had a poor game when every mistake they made is highlighted using video in front of the whole team. It can affect their confidence ahead of the next game and lead to a run of poor performances. A safe environment is where everyone understands that they will all make mistakes at some time, that they will not be judged or blamed for these mistakes, and that analysing the performance in greater detail can lead to improvements in performance. It is also a time for the whole team to discuss ways they can do things better, be more creative and innovative, and improve performance. Some rugby coaches only analyse what went wrong, but it is also important to celebrate and enjoy the positive aspects of performance too, and make sure that the things that went well are also noticed and built on.

These lessons from the world of sport can be easily applied in other working environments. The challenge is to take time, and have the patience and energy to invest in this increasingly important area for success.

CHAPTER 5

ENABLING DIVERSITY AND INCLUSION

'Strength lies in differences, not in similarities.'

Stephen R. Covey, American author and educator

INTRODUCTION

Social movements such as Black Lives Matter, #ME Too and LGBTQ rights have propelled Diversity and Inclusion to the top of organisation's agendas. And it has become an essential part of recruitment too. Nearly 70 per cent of jobseekers now think that diversity is highly important when it comes to choosing an organisation to work for. This suggests that Diversity and Inclusion matters by encouraging a broader perspective on complex issues and more effective outcomes. Appropriate levels of diversity will have a direct effect on your team's performance, its ability to attract and retain talent and on team members' motivation and engagement.

You might have been wondering why these two words – 'Diversity' and 'Inclusion' – are almost always associated. The first thing to point out about Diversity and Inclusion is that they do actually need to go together. Having a diverse team but not being inclusive would not be effective, and similarly, being inclusive but not having any diversity in the team would be kind of pointless. You can think of Diversity as being about the facts – how diverse is your team in terms of age, gender, ethnicity etc.? – and inclusion as being about the choices you make as a team leader and team member to actually *include* these different voices. If your team is diverse but the diverse voices are not listened to, then they are likely to feel that they do not belong and will be disengaged and probably seek to find another organisation that would welcome them and be inclusive of their opinions. As one client told us, 'Diversity is being invited to the dance and inclusion is being invited to dance once you're there'.

Inclusion is what unlocks diversity, according to diversity consultant Jennifer Morris. We often work with teams that are quite diverse but have really low inclusion. One example of what happens when there is a low level of inclusion in the team is that someone makes a suggestion that is not listened to or picked up on. Then someone with a louder voice or more power makes the same or a similar suggestion, which is then picked up and acted upon, but is not credited to the original person. Just having a diverse team is not sufficient. All individuals in the team must feel fully included, respected and listened to. Unfortunately, this is not always the case.

REFLECTION

Before we explore diversity and inclusion any further you might like to reflect about diversity and inclusion in your own organisation, department and team. How would you score each on a scale of 1 to 10 with 1 being poor and 10 being truly diverse? Use the chart below to record you score and make notes as to why.

Diversity in my	Score between 1 and 10	Notes regarding the reasons for your score
Organisation		
Department		
Team		

PERSPECTIVES ON DIVERSITY AND INCLUSION

We can look at Diversity and Inclusion in teams from a few different perspectives. **Firstly**, the legal and regulatory perspective – what does the law in your country say about Diversity and Equality? What do these regulations mean for your team and organisation? This is probably the minimum level – obey the law, but it's not sufficient.

Secondly, the ethical perspective. Isn't it right and proper to be diverse and represent the different diversities that exist? It would be, to say the least, unfair and immoral for the organisation not to be representative. On top of that it would bring specific problems, for example, about credibility, if you are not representative. For example – a purely white, male police force could not legitimately claim to be representative in the UK and would struggle to perform its duties with the consent of a public that it did not represent. Teams that are not representative of their market would struggle to maintain a connection with that market. And there is no doubt that there is a lack of diversity in most organisations. For example, in the USA only 16 per cent of members in executive teams are women, and in the UK this number is only 12 per cent. In the UK, according to Sir John Parker's review into the diversity of FTSE 100 companies (Parker, 2017), only five had women CEOs. When women make up more than half the population of the UK, this is clearly unacceptable.

The **third** perspective is that of creativity, innovation and challenge. The more diverse the team, the more likely you are to get different points of view and perspectives on a specific issue. In a complex world, where there are very few easy answers, taking the time to invite and listen to different voices is highly effective. In research by the Boston Consulting Group in 2014, 75 per cent of executives stated that innovation was among their organisation's top three priorities. But in the same piece of research, 83 per cent stated that their innovation capacities were average or weak. So there is clearly work to do.

Having diversity of thought and perspective leads to a more creative team and more innovative thinking. Clearly this has its own challenges. Decision making might be slower, but in the long run it is better to have a good decision that has been discussed at length, where people have voiced their points of view and concerns and they have been listened to and are therefore more likely to be fully engaged when implemented. There might then be more conflict – but in that case team leaders and team members will have to acquire the skills of conflict resolution. A lack of conflict is not a good thing for a team. If you have complete convergence where there is no diversity, then obviously decisions can be reached more quickly, but you would not have taken account of many different perspectives.

To have diversity of thought you need to have the broadest spectrum of diversity possible. This should include cognitive diversity as well as gender, sexual preference, ethnicity and so on. But as we have already suggested, diversity is often sadly lacking in our institutions. For example, the European Institute for Gender Equality tracked seven areas in which men and women are on average unequal in European Union member states (EIGE, 2021). These areas are – work, money, knowledge, time, power, health and violence. The most current figures are for 2015 and these show that there is a score of 66 per cent for equality between men and women in the EU. At 100 per cent men and women would be equal – so it's evident that men are privileged compared to women in the European Union. And it's even worse in many teams and organisations.

BUILDING AN INCLUSIVE AND DIVERSE CULTURE

Organisations often recruit similar people to themselves – they are looking for a cultural fit rather than thinking about *building* an effective culture. This requires a change of mindset and a focus on *creating* a culture rather than merely seeking to perpetuate an existing culture.

In a *Times* article, journalist Matthew Syed stated that diversity brings different identities, perspectives and insights into the tactics, which leads to better problem solving and outcomes. It's critical when teams are facing complex problems, often called wicked problems, that there are different perspectives in the team, and that they are all heard. With a wicked problem, there are no simple obvious answers to the problem – indeed there are no answers at all – only different options. As Kahneman et al. state in their book *Noise*, 'You want divergence when faced with wicked problems' (Kahneman et al., 2021). The danger is that if the team doesn't have diverse perspectives, everyone is then looking at the issue from the same narrow perspective. If that is the case, then the range of options created can be very limited.

Scott Drawer is a sports scientist who works for Team GB. He recruited a bunch of people who would challenge his thinking (Drawer, 2019).

Michelin-starred chef Tom Kerridge is a keen supporter of diversity: in an interview with us, Tom said the following:

*Kitchens are not full of people who have first class honours degrees. They are normally full of people from society, where it takes all sorts. The way I always describe a kitchen is that it is like a pirate ship: its full of loads of individuals – it's completely eclectic, it's very interesting, it's a melting pot of cultures and backgrounds. Everybody is welcome, all aiming for one thing, cooking, fun, adventure, excitement. They are amazing places to be, and because of the kind of people you attract it's an eclectic and rich mix. (*Personal interview with authors, 2021*)*

Rugby teams have become even more diverse with the advent of the professional game – with players from different cultures and ethnicities – and the teams are all the stronger for that diversity.

WHAT DOES IT MEAN FOR YOU AND YOUR ORGANISATION?

The consulting firm Deloitte has carried out extensive research into diversity and the essential traits that leaders, managers and team members will need in order to deal with the need for diversity.

Deloitte's research showed that there were four mega trends in diversity.

1. **Diversity of markets.** The majority of growth in the middle-class population will come from Asia, Africa and Latin America. If organisations have global ambitions, then they will need people with a more global mindset who are more open to diversity and who are able to attract and retain local talent in these markets.

2. **Diversity of customers.** This is clearly linked to the above because as markets become more diverse then so do the customers. Really effective organisations are working hard to develop more customer-centric mindsets and capacities. Organisations' employees and teams will have to reflect the diversity of their customer base.

3. **Diversity of ideas.** Bill Gates once said that organisations must innovate or die, and innovation is among the top priorities of organisations. The best way to have effective innovation is to promote divergent thinking and to guard against the dangers of group think. This is about harnessing the collective intelligence of the organisation, which means that the organisations' leaders must listen to different points of view and actively encourage challenge.

4. **Diversity of talent.** Successful organisations will be able to develop and optimise a diverse talent pool. To look at the context – by 2030 China will have more graduates than the entire US workforce. There will be a group of highly mobile, well-educated workers and organisations will need to work hard to attract and retain the best talent. Leaders will have to adapt to the different demands of their talent. For example, according to a PWC report (PWC, 2011) millennials already comprise 50 per cent of the global workforce and they have very different expectations and attitudes.

These mega trends are the new context – the context in which we are all now operating. In order to deal effectively with these mega trends, they suggest that there are six key traits that inclusive individuals and leaders must have.

1. **Collaboration.** These are the skills of empowering others, allowing other people's voices to be heard and the ability to create an effective team.

2. **Cultural intelligence.** This is primarily about knowledge of other cultures and preferences and an individual's level of adaptability.

3. **Curiosity.** This is about the degree of openness, ability to take different perspectives and to cope with ambiguity.

4. **Cognisance.** (Awareness) This is a person's degree of self-awareness about their own biases, their ability to control and regulate emotions and how fair they are when dealing with others.

5. **Courage.** This is about showing humility and bravery. Having the courage to challenge entrenched attitudes about diversity and calling out discrimination when you see it. We see this as an especially important trait. If you tolerate casual discrimination, then it becomes the accepted way of doing things. If as a leader, you do not call out and challenge any form of discrimination, then it's highly unlikely that other people will.

6. **Commitment.** This is about sticking with the process of becoming more diverse – which is not always an easy one – and having a strong belief that it is the right thing to do.

REFLECTION

Thinking about these traits, how would you assess yourself and how could you improve in each trait? Use the chart below to note down how you rate yourself on a scale of 1 to 5 with 1 being low and 5 being high. Note down initial ideas on how you can improve.

Trait	Self-rating	Notes on how to improve
Collaboration		
Cultural intelligence		
Curiosity		
Cognisance		
Courage		
Commitment		

Once you have rated yourself and noted down any ideas, you might like to begin prioritising the areas that are the most important in your current context, and how you might start taking specific actions.

Finally, Hunt et al.'s report *Diversity Matters* tells us that companies rated in the top quartile for diversity financially outperform those on the bottom quartile (Hunt et al., 2015). They also attract and retain top talent and have better customer orientation.

As well as looking at diversity from the perspective of gender, race, age, sexual preference and so on, we can also look at it from the perspective of cognitive diversity. Cognitive diversity is defined as differences in perspective or information processing styles. It is not predicted by factors such as gender, ethnicity or age.

Research by our colleagues Alison Reynolds and Dave Lewis (2017) found that a high degree of cognitive diversity could generate accelerated learning and performance in the face of new, uncertain and complex situations. So the lesson is to also look for cognitive diversity as well as other forms of diversity.

WHAT CAN YOU DO?

Here are a few tips on how to increase Diversity and Inclusion within your team.

- The main focus should be in **bringing more diversity** into the team and on **recognising the diversity** that already exists in the team. Take stock of the existing levels of diversity in your team. For instance: people from ethnic minorities make up approximately 13 per cent of the UK population. So, you should be aiming for at least that level of representation on your team. Women make up more than half of the UK population, so you may like to consider whether you should examine the gender balance in your team.

- Be sure you are being **fully inclusive** of all the diversity in the team. Examine any biases that may be present and work hard to allow everyone to express their opinions fully.

- Think about **creating employee networks** in the organisation in order to support diversity. For example, consulting company Lane 4 have several employee networks or forums where people can discuss, share issues, become more aware and educate themselves about various issues connected to Diversity and Inclusion. There is:

  o Mind 4 – for mental health support

  o Black Lives Matter – a network for black and ethnic minority employees

  o Thrive – which is a network for women (but which is open to men).

International construction firm Mace have employee networks such as Women at Mace, Pride at Mace, Parents at Mace, Ethnic Diversity and Inclusion, Enabled at Mace and Mace Military. These networks all create awareness, knowledge and education within the organisation and of course within their teams. But it is essential that top leadership support and encourage these networks.

- **Examine your recruitment practices.** Think of how you word your job advertisements and where you place them. Could the job descriptions be more inclusive? Could you proactively recruit among underrepresented populations?

- **Have clear rules of conduct and behaviour.** Ensure these are respected.

- **Stamp out any discriminatory words and actions.** Don't allow casual discriminatory remarks – insist that team members are respectful of diversity. This is the responsibility of all the team members not just the team boss. The recent case of cricketer Azeem Rafiq illustrates what can happen if you allow a culture of casual racism to exist. Rafiq filed a legal complaint against Yorkshire Cricket Club claiming direct discrimination and harassment on the grounds of race. The 29-year-old, who played professionally for Yorkshire in two spells between 2008 and 2018, also claimed victimisation and detriment as a result of his efforts to address racism at the club. Some of the players that Rafiq accused of racism said that it was simply friendly 'banter'. But clearly telling someone to go back where they came from, or referring to them as 'you lot', is not friendly banter – it is racism pure and simple, and its effect on Rafiq was extremely negative. This kind of language needs to be taken out of a team's culture, and the responsibility lies not just with the top management but with every single player. Don't accept this kind of behaviour in the team – speak up and let it be known that it is unacceptable. Of course this takes courage, but how can you have an effective team if some members are being harassed and are victims because of their race, colour, gender or sexual preference?

  In an interview Rafiq said, 'I want to see kids starting off their journey in cricket in a culture of acceptance and respect, where they are judged on their talent and not on their culture and identity. I hope that the investigation will result in meaningful change at the club and in the sport'.

- **'Know' before you 'do'.** This means taking the time to find out what is happening. Explore people's issues and concerns before you start taking action. Build the actions on what is really happening in the team rather than as a tick box exercise.

The importance of acting effectively in increasing diversity, equality and inclusion in the workforce was recently illustrated by an internal report into the Bank of England's approach to Diversity and Inclusion. It stated that staff from ethnic minority backgrounds were less likely to be promoted, earned less and were more likely to feel they were being treated unfairly than their white colleagues. One of the report's recommendations was that senior managers should be held accountable through their pay packets for meeting inclusion targets. The Governor (the equivalent of the CEO) of the Bank stated that a truly diverse and inclusive bank was 'mission critical' for the organisation. We wonder how many other CEOs would have the same feeling.

CHAPTER 6

WORKING IN VIRTUAL TEAMS

'We like to give people the freedom to work where they want, safe in the knowledge that they have the drive and expertise to perform excellently whether they are at their desk or in their kitchen. Yours truly has never worked out of an office, and never will.'

Richard Branson

INTRODUCTION

Writing this during the pandemic has given us a heightened perspective on the use of virtual teams and virtual meetings. Everything we have written in the book about the basics of good teamwork still applies to working virtually, but we could think of it as working harder at the basics when you are meeting remotely – a sort of fundamentals plus, because things become amplified when working remotely. For example, if you are struggling to understand something in a face-to-face meeting, you might very well ask a trusted colleague to help you as you are leaving the meeting. This kind of informal communication isn't so easy when working remotely.

REMOTE WORKING – GOOD PRACTICES

There are clearly advantages and disadvantages to having virtual meetings, but it is our opinion that the most important thing is to stick to some key good practices when the team is functioning remotely. These practices are outlined below.

Create a sense of psychological safety. We've written about this in Chapter 4 but we feel it becomes even more important for the team to have a strong sense of psychological safety when working virtually and remotely.

Pay attention to relationship and emotions. There can be a focus when meeting virtually on purely technical and functional aspects of the work to the detriment of participants' emotional states and the quality of the relationships.

Allow people to network. When we are in the office, we bump into people at the water cooler or coffee machine or in the canteen and reinforce relationships and swap stories and ideas. We might informally ask for some help or another colleague's perspectives on a tricky issue we are facing. There are different ways of doing this virtually. You can create catch up/get together virtual sessions. One company we know asked meeting participants to give a virtual tour of their workplace during the pandemic and also did a talent show to help bring people together and have some fun. You could ask your colleagues to give the team a virtual tour of their workplace so everyone can get a sense of where you are having to work.

Or even more simply – open up meetings 20 minutes or so early so people can chat informally before the formal session.

Check in. Before going straight to business, it's vital to take a few minutes to hear from everyone in the meeting – to get everyone's voice in the room and not just the extravert's. Hear from everyone as to what is going on for them at the moment and how they are feeling. What we have seen is that too many meetings are lacking the human element and taking account of people's feelings and emotions. We are social animals, and we need to keep a strong sense of relationship alive in the virtual setting.

Contracting and charter. We believe that clear contracting is especially important in virtual meetings. The contracting part is around why are we coming together in this meeting and what is the purpose. Also, it's a good idea to have some clear rules and guidelines for virtual meetings so that everyone is on the same page. That could include guidelines on using the camera, not allowing multitasking, using the chat box and the various icons.

Be aware of your presence in virtual meetings. We said earlier that everything can get amplified in the virtual space so it's important to remain focused and present in the meeting. So do not try to multitask while you are in a virtual meeting. People will notice that you are not being fully present.

Have a buddy system. If you have large-scale virtual events, create a buddy system where you link two participants together so that they can support, encourage and make sense of what's happened in a more intimate and safe space by using break out rooms for discussions.

Ensure everyone understands the technical aspects. This has been a particular bugbear during the Covid pandemic as it's obvious that many team members have not been helped to get up to speed on how to work with Zoom or Teams or whatever platform your organisation is using. Not everyone understands the instructions in the IT department's email – so make sure you offer individual help to everyone attending a virtual meeting. This includes helping with the basics of finding a quiet space, using a headphone set, quality of sound as well as using the additional functionality like chat, mood buttons, hand up and break out rooms.

However, there are some drawbacks emerging in relation to virtual working. These include:

- lack of informal social interaction
- challenges in developing 'team' spirit and cohesion

- little opportunity for spontaneous meetings and conversations, by the coffee machine for example
- lack of awareness of the challenges some team members face in their working practises, for instance inadequate workspace in the home, young families running around in the background and so on
- feelings of social isolation which can affect overall health and well-being
- feelings of resentment that individuals have to supply their own office furniture (often not ergonomically satisfactory) as well as the other costs involved in working from home.

These drawbacks need to be carefully considered when deciding what your policies will be regarding virtual working. Organisations, teams and their leaders must take into account the needs and preferences of all the relevant stakeholders before rushing into making decisions about the way ahead for virtual working practises in your business.

TEN TOP TIPS

Here are ten key tips and ideas on how to make the most of virtual meetings inspired by our colleague Dr Ghislaine Caulat who has been researching virtual working for almost 15 years.

1. Try to keep the use of PowerPoint slides to a minimum. It's ok to use them in a training session as a reminder but the general principle is to send any slides out in advance along with some specific questions. Then use the time in the meeting for ensuring understanding, clarification and decision making.

2. Don't speak for more than 4 minutes without asking a question or bringing others in.

3. Use simultaneous meeting minutes so that everyone can see what has been agreed. This increases understanding and also commitment.

4. Forget the usual teleconference etiquette. For example, people don't have to say their name when they speak, they don't have to put themselves on mute (unless they have a noisy background) and it's ok to interrupt skilfully. This sounds counter intuitive, but it increases spontaneity. Allow people to speak up and ask for a break if they need one. They will disappear anyway so you might as well allow everyone to take a moment to get a drink, use the bathroom or get

up and move about. We have seen so many meetings where the team leader goes on endlessly without interruption. They may have a cast iron bladder and no need to rehydrate, but not everyone else does!

5. Don't go straight into the formal agenda. Take time to establish the human connection by asking people to share what's going on in their world, how they are feeling and what might be important to them in the meeting. This also gives everyone in the meeting the chance to be heard, which is really important. If people don't speak up early, then it's much more difficult to speak up later in the meeting. If you don't do this there will be meetings where some people have not been heard at all. Clearly this is counterproductive.

6. Don't be afraid of silence. Silence tends to be over amplified in virtual meetings so that what might be seen as a moment of quiet reflection in a face-to-face meeting becomes something awkward in the virtual space. But don't rush to fill it, normalise the silence by saying something like 'I'm noticing that we have been silent for the last minute or so. Help me understand what this silence is telling us'. In Ghislaine's words *'Feel it don't fill it!'*. Linked to this is how to deal with introverts and extraverts. Don't make the mistake of asking the team, *'What do you think?'* because the extraverts will immediately tell you what they think! Say something like, *'Some of us have been vocal in the meeting and can I ask them to be silent for a moment and invite the quieter people to share their perspective'?*

7. Pay attention to the hygiene factors: make sure people are calling in from a quiet background. Use headsets that cover both ears. Don't mix virtual and face-to-face meetings. Avoid HQcentricity. This is where the people in the organisation's HQ set the times for meetings to suit themselves. But if you are having virtual meetings where people are calling in from all over the world, make sure that HQ sometimes has to get up early or stay late. Create a scheduling table which specifies the times that everyone has to attend the meeting so that this is obvious to everyone.

8. Do not do back-to-back virtual meetings, where for example you have a 9.00 am call which finishes at 10.00 and then you have scheduled a 10.00 am meeting. Get into the habit of scheduling meetings for 45- or 50-minutes' duration. This allows some down time between meetings for planning, reflecting, preparing and moving about before the next virtual call.

9. Think of the specific roles that need to happen in a virtual meeting. You can have the Leader, the person who calls the meeting. Another role is the Facilitator whose job it might be to take minutes and pay attention to the dynamics of the meeting. Another role might be that of Carer – the person who focuses on time management and helping people to get back into the meeting if their connection is broken.

10. Finally – think of your impact and presence in the virtual meeting. How are you presenting yourself? How does your voice sound? How do others hear you? Think of the energy you are bringing and your posture and make sure you have everything you need to hand like water, coffee and even some food.

CHAPTER 7

INFLUENCING IN A TEAM ENVIRONMENT

'Effective leadership involves influencing others so that they are motivated to contribute to the achievement of group goals.'

Haslam, Reicher and Platow (2011)

INTRODUCTION

For us, influencing is an essential part of the team leadership process and indeed for any person in organisational life. We believe that to lead is in fact to influence. Recent research echoes this and confirms that leadership is about achieving influence, not securing compliance. Studies done by Mike and Fiona, the Hay Group and many others have concluded that in the future leaders will have to manage through influence rather than by using authority. As a team leader or team member you will need to be able to influence ethically and effectively. You will find many situations in which you have to influence, whether it is influencing the team collectively, or individual team members, or other people and teams on behalf of your team.

WHAT DO WE MEAN BY INFLUENCE?

It is important to be clear about what influencing is and what it is not. We are often asked what the difference is between the words:

- influencing
- persuading
- convincing.

The terms are often used interchangeably, but there are some key differences. Persuasion always involves influencing but influence does not always involve persuasion. In other words, you can influence by other means than persuasion: for example, you can influence people unconsciously, by the way you speak or dress or by your posture.

In the table below we offer a summary of the meanings of influencing, persuading and convincing. We have also added in the word 'manipulation', which is a negative aspect of influence and is another word people often ask us about.

	Our Definitions
Influence	To get movement in another person's position
Persuade	To urge someone strongly
Convince	When the influencee moves fully towards the influencer's position
Manipulate	To influence deviously

The chart below illustrates our definition of influencing.

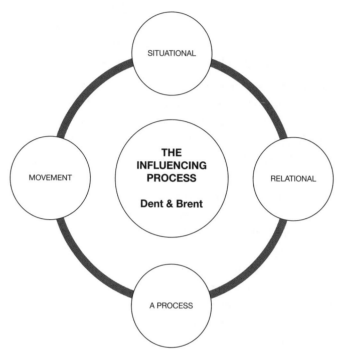

The influencing process

The influencing process is **Situational**, in that how you influence depends on the context in which you are influencing. It is **Relational** in the sense that you are always influencing other people, and therefore need to have good emotional and relational intelligence. It is also mostly a **Process** rather than a one-off event. This implies that you are likely to be influencing over a period of time and therefore you can sometimes afford to influence in small steps rather than try to immediately convince. Finally, for us influencing is about **Movement**. That means if you get some movement in the other person's position then you have successfully influenced someone. When you are influencing without formal authority, it's far more likely that you will achieve some movement in the other person's position rather than expect to convince someone 100 per cent.

HOW DO PEOPLE LIKE TO BE INFLUENCED?

It is thought provoking to look into how people actually like to be influenced. Over several years we have researched with hundreds of managers how they liked to be influenced and also what acted as influencing turnoffs. The results were interesting and listed below are the main categories.

- **Involvement.** The managers said that to be influenced effectively they needed to be involved. They wanted to be listened to, and their opinions and perspectives to be taken into account.

- **Confidence.** There was a desire among influencees for the influencer to demonstrate confidence and positivity as well as energy and conviction about the issue.

- **Appreciation.** People want to be appreciated for their contributions. This can be done by developing rapport and building a relationship that is mutually beneficial and based on likeability. Having a positive relationship with others means they are more likely to listen to you.

- **Credibility.** Managers told us that influencers need to establish a certain credibility. This can be achieved by having a good reputation and of course sound knowledge and a good track record.

- **Evidence.** There was a strong need for sound arguments, logic and data to support the influencing case. If possible, the influencer should bring in any relevant research and data to back up their argument.

- **Clarity.** Managers told us that they liked clarity and wanted influencers to be articulate but concise. They hated 'waffle' and beating about the bush.

- **Passion.** The expectation is that as an influencer you will demonstrate a level of passion and energy about the idea which, in turn, will indicate self-belief and confidence.

You might like to think about the above areas and assess yourself in terms of whether or not this is an area you use when influencing. Use the chart below to rate yourself 1 to 10 with 1 being not an area I use and 10 being use it all the time. You should also make notes about how you use these categories, how you can use them more and for those you do not use think about why and how you might use them.

REFLECTION

Influencing Exercise		
Category	Score	Notes
Involvement		
Confidence		
Appreciation		
Credibility		
Evidence		
Clarity		
Passion		

In terms of what turned them off and made influencers ineffective the managers identified five main reasons:

- **Being patronised:** managers felt that influencers who were condescending towards them was a real turnoff.

- **Being put under pressure:** it was felt that being put under pressure to do something or using 'hard sell' tactics was counterproductive.

- **Using authority:** the exclusive use of formal or position power was viewed as somewhat ineffective. It was felt that if someone could not convince them with good reasons and had to resort to their formal authority, then they had failed. They might have to comply but would not be convinced.

- **Asking for, then discounting ideas:** this was a major turnoff. It happens when people *appear* to ask for your thoughts but then go on to completely disregard them.

- **Feeling manipulated:** this is when managers felt that they are being deceived and misled. They might initially have been influenced but when they realise they had been misled, any influence is destroyed.

These ideas were expressed by a broad range of managers and leaders who work at all levels in organisational life and in many different roles and professions. In summary it seems to us that when being influenced people want three key things – **Involvement, Clarity and Authenticity**.

THE USE OF FORMAL AND INFORMAL AUTHORITY

To get things done in the team, the team leader and its members have two options. One is to use formal authority; the other is to use a more informal authority, which we describe as influencing without authority. Another way of looking at this is asking yourself whether you want **compliance** or **commitment**?

People will not do what you want if they don't know what you want – so there is a clear basis for at least communicating what you want. You can do this in two ways. One is to tell or order people to do what you want. This may work for some people in some organisations, some of the time, but generally it's not an effective way of getting things done any more. And even if you do use this approach to gain compliance with your ideas there are skilled and unskilled ways of doing it (more on this later).

So how do you get things done if you don't tell people? You need to get their commitment to doing something they perhaps were not originally going to do, in other words you are going to try to influence them to see things from your perspective. This is when you are influencing without authority.

A further argument in favour of using a more involving influencing style rather than a command or tell one is that it builds sustainable team leadership. When you order someone to do something, you are building in the necessity to keep on giving orders, and if you rely too much on formal power you run the risk of team members simply doing what they are told. You might obtain compliance, but you won't achieve the team's commitment, where team members will feel more involved and appreciated, and therefore perform better.

Use of formal power in a team environment is neither effective nor efficient. Control leads in the end to dependency, but by using a more involving influencing approach you devolve power to the influencee. This of course implies that the influencer must be open to being influenced. If you only ever want to be the influencer, then you are commanding and telling, but under a different name! In effect, a large part of the team leader's job is to discuss things with colleagues, peers and bosses, and is not just about the simple delivery of orders to team members. In this type of situation, negotiating or influencing skills become paramount, because the option of using formal power is no longer effective or efficient. In his work as a team captain and team coach, Nigel recognised that effective and skilful influencing is a key aspect of effective team leadership, but because influencing is such a critical skill, we believe that each member of a team must develop the skills to influence stakeholders effectively.

REFLECTION

Before we move on to examining the four influencing approaches, you may find it useful to reflect about the people you have to influence on a regular basis – your team members, colleagues, bosses, customers, and so on.

We find using a mind mapping technique very effective to collect and note down information about each person, which will help you to determine how best to influence them – in most situations this will mean different approaches for each person. It is this that makes influencing a complex and time-consuming process. However, the more you prepare, the more efficient you will become. So, knowing what might work for each person you have to influence will lead to greater effectiveness in the long term.

Start with a blank sheet of paper and create a mind map similar to the one in the chart below by focussing on one particular influencing issue.

Firstly, write down the issue in the centre of your sheet.

Annotate your map by writing down the key stakeholders either by category – boss, colleagues, team, clients, and so on or by name.

Prioritise the people in terms of their importance in relation to the issue – use a code for instance A, B, C. . . .

This is now your basic mind map and you can move onto the steps suggested below.

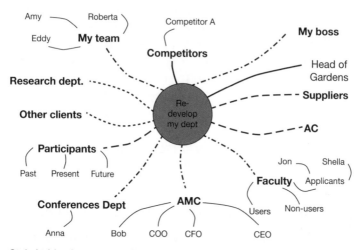

Stakeholders' map example: key stakeholders

On the previous page is an example of a real mind map created by Mike when he was leading the Ashridge Experiential Learning Team.

Once you have your basic mind map showing all the people you have to influence on a regular basis, you can decide on the most critical and then annotate it with useful information to help you adapt your influencing approach, such as:

- What motivates and demotivates each person?
- Is the person a key influencer in their own right? What are the implications?
- Is it someone you like or dislike? And why?
- Are they easy or difficult to work with? What makes them easy or difficult?
- What is your relationship with this person like? Use a scale of 1 = poor to 10 = excellent to evaluate each relationship and identify how you might improve them.
- Do they prefer detail or are they more strategic?
- What things do you have in common?

You can then use this information to inform your influencing tactics and strategies. Ideally your influencing tactics will vary for each different person you need to influence. In the example above which Mike created when he wanted to re-develop the experiential learning department in Ashridge, he needed to influence several key stakeholders. By identifying their different needs and areas of interests Mike was able to frame his influencing more effectively. Influencing the CEO was different to influencing the CFO for example. The CFO needed details and costings which Mike did not have initially. Creating the stakeholder map allowed Mike to reflect more deeply on what making an effective case would be like for each person.

Now we will move on to explore four approaches to influencing which will help you to reflect even more on what approaches and strategies to use.

FOUR APPROACHES TO INFLUENCING

Our research shows us that people use four main approaches to influencing others, as illustrated in the chart below. These are assertive, participative, logical and, finally, inspirational.

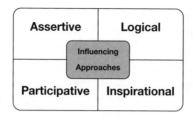

Assertive	Logical
Influencing Approaches	
Participative	Inspirational

Ideally you will be able to skilfully use all of these approaches depending on the needs of the situation. In practice we find that most people have a preference for one, or perhaps two of these approaches, and often find at least one of the approaches difficult to use. For instance: a manager might have a preference for logical and participative approaches, be able to use assertive if necessary and have inspirational influencing as their least preferred approach.

- **Assertive influencer** – you influence in a straightforward and confident way, expressing what you want clearly.

- **Logical influencer** – you influence by presenting your case using reasoning and evidence.

- **Participative influencer** – you influence by involving and engaging interpersonally with others.

- **Inspirational influencer** – you influence by arousing enthusiasm, passion and engaging others' emotions.

In the chart below we have summarised some of the key words associated with each approach.

Assertive	Participative	Logical	Inspirational
Telling	Involve	Facts	Vision
Power	Listen	Analysis	Narrative
Pressure	Appreciate	Detail	Metaphors
Confidence	Inquire	Proof	Symbols
Fast paced	Build on others' ideas	Reason	Energy
Persistent	Use 'Yes, and'	Evidence	Images
Authoritative	Charm	Lack of emotion	Future orientation

Source: Brent and Dent (2010) *The Leader's Guide to Influence*. FT Pearson.

It is important, therefore, for you to understand your own preferred influencing approach and to be aware of your team members' preferences as well. Then you will be able to choose the most effective influencing approach for your team members. One simple way of getting an initial idea of your preferred style would be to use the table above and select the word from each row that best describes your influencing approach – the style with the most selected words might then be your preference. By identifying your strongest preference, you will also identify the areas where you can further develop your influencing style for greater flexibility and effectiveness. The truly skilled influencer will be able to assess a situation and adopt the approach or approaches that will best work for the situation and people involved. This could involve using a range of approaches, moving seamlessly from say, inspiration to participative to logical all-in-one conversation. Nigel says, *'As a coach I always found that my players would respond to a combination of influencing approaches'.*

TOOLS AND TECHNIQUES

There are a huge number of influencing tools and techniques that the team leader can use. Mike and Fiona wrote extensively about these in their book, *The Leader's Guide to Influence* (Brent and Dent, 2010). In this chapter we will focus on a few very effective tools. The chart below indicates those we will discuss.

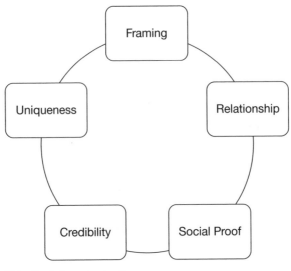

Effective influencing tools

Framing. Frames are the mental structures that allow us to understand reality – and sometimes to create what we take to be reality. A frame is a set of assumptions or beliefs about a situation. For example, influencer A might believe that good teamwork is getting the team to agree with her thoughts. But for influencer B, good teamwork might be getting everyone in the team sharing a collective vision and purpose. Each person here has created their own frame in terms of good teamwork, and clearly this will lead to different behaviours.

So, it's about how we manage the meaning of an interaction with someone, focusing on the perspective you want to share with the others. It is therefore clearly important to understand how you are framing a situation, and how your colleagues are framing it. You will also need to know how to *reframe* effectively in order to influence.

For instance, let's say someone in your team is underperforming and you start to think of them as a 'problem performer'. You are in effect framing them as a problem and the danger is that if you continue to frame them as a problem, then that will affect how you behave towards them. The concern is that your behaviour towards them simply reinforces the situation, because you are more likely to be short tempered with them and ignore any positive aspects of their behaviour. What you can try to do is to *reframe* the situation by looking at when the person has **NOT** been a poor performer, and by looking at something that this team member does well. You are then more likely to be appreciative of these things and start asking questions about the perceived poor performance in a calm, non-judgmental way. Reframing your perspective in this way enables your colleague to refocus their energy and efforts in a constructive way.

There are many ways of reframing. The simplest and most obvious example of reframing is the glass half full, glass half empty analogy. Framing the glass as half empty focuses on what you don't have, whereas framing it as half full focuses on what you have.

When you reframe a situation, you are trying to look at it from a different and more useful perspective. For example, in an influencing situation, we usually frame the situation from our own perspective. It might be more influential to try framing it from the influencee's perspective. This is what we call the 'SWIIFT' perspective – *'So what's in it for them?'*

You can help your colleagues learn and develop by using this framing technique with them, and it can be used to influence yourself as well as others. If they fail at something, they might become despondent and de-energised, because failure is usually framed as a bad thing and is to be avoided. But you could help them reframe their failure as learning by asking effective questions such as: 'What did you learn from the failure?' 'What were your assumptions about the situation?' 'What can you do differently in future?'

REFRAMING EXAMPLE

The American inventor Thomas Edison was famously quoted as saying, 'Every wrong attempt is another step forward. I have not failed 10,000 times, I have successfully found 10,000 ways that will not work'. *This attitude helped him to invent, among other things, the phonograph, the first commercially viable electric light bulb and the motion picture camera.*

Relationship. Relationship is about empathy, liking and trust. If you have no formal authority over someone and they don't like or trust you, then you will have great difficulty in influencing them. However, if you have a positive relationship and a high degree of trust, then it's far more likely that you will be able to influence them. This of course implies that you need to think strategically about your relationships, both inside and outside the team. You can make a list of your colleagues and then rate the quality of your relationship with each person on a scale of 1 to 10, 10 being excellent. That is not to say that you need to have a perfect-10 relationship but if it's less than a 5 you probably need to focus some effort on building or rebuilding the relationship with that colleague.

Some of the things you can do to improve the relationship is to be empathetic and appreciative towards other people and focus more on what they do well rather than feeling the need to be critical. Research tells us that it's more effective in terms of performance to:

- listen more than you tell
- be more focused on your team colleagues than yourself
- share more positive and appreciative feedback than criticisms.

Relationship is also linked to emotion, and it is important to remember that being right about something does not necessarily mean you have influenced anyone.

Social proof. We are the third most social species on the planet – after ants and bees – and so we are hugely influenced by what other people think and do, especially people who are similar to us or whom we admire and respect. It therefore makes sense when you are influencing others to try to identify the most popular or respected people and start by influencing them. If you get them on board first, then it will be much easier to influence the others.

An example of social proof in influencing is when you see buskers or street performers passing round the hat. They will always either seed the hat (i.e. put some money in it first) and/or ensure that a colleague or friendly member of the audience steps up and puts in some money (preferably paper money, not coins).

When influencing your team, make sure you use examples that are relevant. You might want to adopt a particular process – so if the team likes sport, you might use the New Zealand All Blacks rugby team as an example of a successful team who already use this process successfully. Be careful, however, to make sure that your example of social proof does actually resonate with the people you are influencing.

Credibility. If you are not seen as someone who is credible, then it will be extremely difficult to influence without recourse to formal authority. It therefore becomes important to think about your credibility and your reputation or how your colleagues see you. If you are seen as having lots of expertise and credibility in an area, then it becomes much easier to influence effectively. The question then is how do you enhance your credibility and authority? This will depend on the makeup of the team of people you work with, and what they consider as credible. For some fast-paced sales teams, your credibility will depend on your sales ability, for other teams it might rest on your experience and expertise, and for others, your empathy and relational skills.

REFLECTION

How would you describe your reputation? Where does your credibility come from? It is also critical to give some thought to your image and reputation and ensure that it is positive.

Uniqueness. What distinguishes one product or service, or indeed one person from another, is how distinctive or unique you are. Although we realise that every human being is unique, it is a fact that some stand out from the crowd more than others.

The big danger for products or services is that they might be seen as a commodity, and therefore be considered less valuable. So how does an organisation differentiate itself? If you have for example ten estate agencies on your high street, how do you choose which one to use? The answer is differentiation. Which one is the friendliest? Which one is the most efficient? Which one has the best customer service? Which one can you trust?

Although we as humans cannot ever be seen as commodities, there is a danger that when influencing we are not seen as being unique enough and are therefore less effective as influencers. So, the question becomes, 'What makes you different?' 'What is your USP?' (unique selling point). One way of being more unique is to tell a story. Humans are natural storytellers and stories resonate with us in a much more compelling way than pure logic, so try to create a story and a narrative rather than just giving the facts. Professor Mark Turner, in his book, *The Literary Mind* (1996), wrote that most of our experience, our knowledge and our thinking is organised as stories.

The essential difference between reason and emotion according to Canadian neurologist Donald Calne (2010) is that reason leads to conclusions, whereas emotion leads to action. This means that you will need to bring in an emotional element to your influencing. Telling a story rather than just sharing facts and figures is an effective way to bring emotion into your influencing.

Finally, influencing is a two-way process. As an influencer you need to be able to influence people but also be open to being influenced. To influence effectively means using tools, principles and techniques such as we have described above, in a skilful, appropriate, flexible and ethical way.

CHAPTER 8

ENGAGING THE TEAM

'Engaged employees are psychological "owners", drive performance and innovation, and move the organisation forward.'

Gallup Report, 2017

INTRODUCTION

The subject of how important engaged team members are to the team and the organisation is of much interest and research. It is considered so important that most major organisations carry out regular engagement surveys to gauge the level of engagement among their employees. This chapter will explore concrete ways of ensuring higher engagement in the team.

WHY IS ENGAGEMENT IMPORTANT TO THE TEAM?

A number of studies have demonstrated significant benefits from high levels of engagement. Some of the findings are that high engagement leads to:

- higher revenue growth, productivity, profitability and safety for the team and their organisation
- better physical and mental health for team members
- lower absence rates in the team
- lower staff turnover and intention to leave organisation
- higher organisational commitment.

These are all clearly things to aspire to in your team, but how can teams and their leaders ensure that engagement is present?

WHAT IS ENGAGEMENT?

As you might expect there is no clear agreement as to exactly what engagement actually is. According to David MacLeod, engagement is *'About how we create the conditions in which employees offer more of their capability and potential'*. MacLeod is co-author (with Nita Clarke) of the report 'Engaging for success', also known as the MacLeod Report, which was commissioned by the UK Secretary of State for Business in 2008.

There are several other perspectives on what engagement means, but the one that we find the most practical – because it starts to describe some specific behaviours – is one we might loosely describe as the HR perspective. This involves the following four behaviours.

- **Organisational commitment** – you have a level of desire to stay within the organisation. It means that you are not looking to leave in the short term, that you are willing to invest in the team and the organisation and that you are not on the lookout for the next team or company to join.

■ **The willingness to go the extra mile** – you make efforts to go beyond what is normally expected of you. If you just do what you are meant to do or paid to do or what it says in the rule book, you might still be a fairly good team member, but we can't say that you are highly engaged in the team. This question is commonly used in engagement surveys. For example, in one international company, nearly 90 per cent of staff surveyed in one country expressed their willingness to go the extra mile, but in another country only 60 per cent said they would. This allows the company to explore what is being done well in the first country, learn specific lessons and then look at how they might be applied to the other country. They might also find a correlation with other measures such as retention, profitability and so on.

■ **Extra role behaviour** – this is when you don't just stick with the defined roles in the team but go beyond your role in order to help a client or colleague. If team members stick to their specific roles and refuse to go beyond them – even in urgent cases – this tends to indicate a low level of engagement.

■ **Discretionary effort** – this is where you promote the effective functioning of your team or organisation. In other words, you make an effort that you don't have to, or are even expected to do, and might not even be rewarded for, but it helps the team or client.

Thinking about the four behaviours above, you might like to assess yourself against them and make any relevant notes about why this is the case. Use the chart below.

REFLECTION

My Team Engagement Analysis		
Behaviour	Score out of 5 (1 low–5 high)	Notes
My level of organisational commitment		
My willingness to go the extra mile		
My extra role behaviour		
My willingness to put in discretionary effort		

You can also use this quick analysis to assess your team members' levels of engagement.

Another interesting and helpful way of defining engagement is given by Dr Amy Armstrong and her colleagues at Hult Business School. She defines it as: *'An organisational climate where people choose to give the very best of themselves at work'* (Armstrong et al., 2018). Their research found that people fell into four different zones when it came to the level of engagement. See the model that follows.

These zones are:

- Contentment (21 per cent of teams studied)
- Pseudo-engagement (22 per cent of teams studied)
- Disengagement (32 per cent of teams studied)
- Engagement (25 per cent of teams studied).

In the **Zone of Contentment**, things aren't too bad – people are somewhat satisfied, the climate is positive, the team is established yet resistant to change. Team members fulfil their roles, but they are not necessarily close to other team members and are happy for the leader to take responsibility and accountability for the team's performance. This is not a highly engaged team yet functions effectively. Nigel suggests that in a sporting context the team could be described as mid-table mediocrity, happy to not face the challenges of being relegated but never challenging to win the competition.

Pseudo-Engagement is an interesting concept – 22 per cent of teams in the study were located in the Zone of Pseudo-Engagement. To their organisations these teams might appear highly engaged. However, when studied in detail, a range of team dysfunctions are apparent. The climate in pseudo-engaged teams could be described as Machiavellian. With low levels of trust and cohesion, team members are 'out for themselves'. They are proactive, but only in order to serve their own needs, for example by stretching the workload to fill time.

Team members may be engaged individually; however, they do not pull together as a team. There is little evidence of collegiality or support for one another. Team leaders in pseudo-engaged teams may be proactive in giving feedback, but it is often the negatives that are pointed out rather than any positives. Pseudo-engaged teams are unlikely to take responsibility or accountability for their results and quick to blame the leader to protect their own positions. A pseudo-engaged team will work well together as long as results are positive. If there is a run of poor results the team will be quick to blame each other and their coach or leader, and results will continue to decline, and change will be inevitable.

	POSITIVE	NEGATIVE
REACTIVE	**ZONE OF CONTENTMENT** - TEAM LIKES SET WAYS OF WORKING. - LONGER-SERVING TEAM MEMBERS CAN BE RESISTANT TO CHANGE. - PROBLEMS ARE ESCALATED TO TEAM LEADER TO SOLVE. - TRAINING AND DEVELOPMENT IS OVERLOOKED. - TEAM MEMBERS NOT ENCOURAGED TO STEP UP OR TAKE ON NEW CHALLENGES. - TEAM LACKS ENERGY AND ENTHUSIASM. - SOME TEAM MEMBERS ARE HOLDING OUT FOR RETIREMENT. - MOST PEOPLE ARE THERE JUST TO EARN A WAGE. - LITTLE APPETITE TO DO MORE THAN WHAT THE JOB REQUIRES. - TEAM MEMBERS ARE NOT CLOSE TO EACH OTHER. - TEAM MEMBERS COMPLAIN IF ASKED TO WORK OUTSIDE OF CONTRACTED HOURS. - TEAM DOES COME UP WITH NEW WAYS OF DOING THINGS. - TEAM LEADER FINDS IT DIFFICULT TO STEP BACK AND DELEGATE.	**ZONE OF ENGAGEMENT** - WORK TOGETHER TO SOLVE PROBLEMS. - ACTIVELY LOOK FOR SOLUTIONS. - CHALLENGED AND STRETCHED IN THE TEAM. - TEAM DIVERSITY. - POSITIVE ROLE MODELS TO LEARN FROM. - MISTAKES ARE SEEN AS POSITIVE OPPORTUNITIES FOR LEARNING. - TEAM MEMBERS FEEL EMPOWERED, VALUED AND SUPPORTED. - TIGHTLY KNIT TEAM THAT HAVE EACH OTHER'S BACKS. - GO ABOVE AND BEYOND WHAT IS EXPECTED. - FUN ATMOSPHERE. - RESPECT DISAGREEMENT AND DIFFERENCE. - SHARED BELIEF THAT TOGETHER TEAM CAN ACHIEVE ANYTHING. - SEE THE BIGGER PICTURE SO KNOW WHERE THEY FIT IN.
	ZONE OF DISENGAGEMENT - CLIQUES AND GOSSIP ARE RIFE. - BLAME CULTURE. - LOW LEVELS OF TRUST AMONG TEAM MEMBERS. - THERE IS TENSION AND FRICTION AMONG TEAM MEMBERS. - TEAM LEADER IS NOT RESPECTED. - TEAM MEMBERS FEEL UNAPPRECIATED. - WORK IS BORING (MONOTONOUS). - TEAM LEADER IS TOO CONTROLLING AND DOES NOT LEAD BY EXAMPLE. - TEAM MEMBERS DO NOT FEEL LISTENED TO AND FEEL UNABLE TO INFLUENCE. - SOME PEOPLE ARE TREATED DIFFERENTLY THAN OTHERS. - WE DO NOT ALWAYS GET GIVEN INFORMATION. - MEMBERS DO NOT FEEL THEY CAN BE HONEST ABOUT EACH OTHER.	**ZONE OF PSEUDO-ENGAGEMENT** - COLLECTION OF INDIVIDUALS WHO HAPPEN TO WORK TOGETHER. - INDIVIDUALS SERVE OWN NEEDS RATHER THAN THOSE OF THE TEAM. - INDIVIDUALS DO NOT GO OUT OF THEIR WAY TO HELP EACH OTHER. - LITTLE 'TOGETHERNESS' (COLLEGIALITY). - IN FEEDBACK THE NEGATIVES ARE STRESSED MORE THAN THE POSITIVES. - TEAM MEMBERS CAN BE PLAYED OFF AGAINST ONE ANOTHER. - POOR PERFORMANCE IS TOLERATED. - WORK IS SO BUSY, THERE IS NO TIME TO BUILD RELATIONSHIPS. - INDIVIDUALS SAY AND DO THE RIGHT THINGS TO GET INTO THE MANAGERS' 'GOOD BOOKS'. - TEAM LEADER IS MORE INTERESTED IN INGRATIATING THEMSELVES TO SENIOR MANAGEMENT THAN CARING ABOUT US.

TEAM CLIMATE / **TEAM BEHAVIOURS**

PROACTIVE

Armstrong, Oliver & Wilkinson, 2018

© Ashridge Executive Education 2017

In the **Zone of Disengagement** there is no respect for leadership, and little accountability or responsibility for the team's results. With low levels of trust, a culture of blame, no enthusiasm or commitment to their work, the team cannot function effectively. It's only a matter of time before the team is held to account, changed or disbanded completely. When you read about the manager of a football team 'losing the dressing room', it means the team have moved into the Zone of Disengagement.

The **Zone of Engagement** is the zone every leader and organisation would like their teams to be in. Teams in the engagement zone will be challenged and work collaboratively; they will value each other's input, respect their leader and will do whatever it takes to achieve their goals. In sport, it is the engaged teams that challenge for silverware. These are the teams that work together to raise the bar and achieve success.

Based on the research and using Dr Armstrong's list of characteristics we have developed a checklist to help you reflect about and assess where your own team/s are in relation to these zones.

Focus on one team at a time and complete the review by indicating with an x which characteristics are features of your team. Once you have completed the whole chart you will be able to assess which zone your team is in, that is the column with the most 'x's. Once you have established in which zone the team is, you can start to help your team become more engaged.

REFLECTION

Team Engagement Review				
	Col 1			Col 2
Team has set ways of working		Team sees bigger picture		
Team members are not close		There is a fun atmosphere		
Team members have low energy or enthusiasm		Collaborative working is common		
Training and Development is overlooked		The team is diverse		
Members only do as much as required		Members are valued and empowered		
Team leader has difficulty delegating		Team will go the extra mile		
There is no encouragement to take on challenges		The team feels challenged and stretched		
There is a high degree of resistance to change		Mistakes are viewed as opportunities for learning		
Total			Total	

	Col 3		Col 4
A blame culture prevails		Team leader is a boss pleaser	
There are low levels of trust in team		No feeling of collegiality within team	
The team leader is not respected		More positive than negative feedback given	
Little honesty between team members		Team members do the right things to get into bosses' good books	
Team have feelings of boredom		Team is just a group of people who work together	
There is a lack of appreciation in team		Team members compete with each other	
Team leader is controlling		The focus is on task not relationships	
Cliques and gossip are rife in team		Poor performance is tolerated	
Total		Total	
Column 1 Total	Column 2 Total	Column 3 Total	Column 4 Total

Add up the number of 'x's you have in each column – the maximum is 8. Obviously, the highest number of 'x's represents the zone your team is in at the moment. If you have only one or two 'x's in a particular zone, then your team will not be in that zone so that will not be of concern – unless of course you have a low number in column 2. The idea is to move the team into zone 2 – the Zone of Engagement.

Column 1	Column 2	Column 3	Column 4
Zone of Contentment	Zone of Engagement	Zone of Disengagement	Zone of Pseudo-Engagement

Once you have an indication of the zone that most reflects your team you can begin to think about what you might do to continue to improve and develop the engagement levels. We point out a number of ideas on how to do this in the rest of the chapter.

A starting point might be to make a list of the main things you should focus on to maintain and continue to develop the engagement levels in your team. Then focus on three or four specific areas you might work on with your team to help all members become more engaged.

In an ideal world the team should operate mostly in the Zone of Engagement. However, this is something to continually work towards. The key point is to avoid having a team that operates exclusively in the Contentment or Pseudo Team or Disengagement zone.

THREE STEPS TO ENGAGEMVENT

Our own perspective on team engagement, gained from working with hundreds of teams and thousands of team members over a combined period of more than 90 years, is that engagement largely comes from three things – **Purpose, Involvement and Appreciation.**

PURPOSE

It is more and more accepted that for team members to be fully engaged, they need to share a strong sense of purpose and meaning. Staff will engage with organisations and teams that provide clarity around the purpose, goals and anticipated outcomes of their work. Engaged team members believe that achieving these outcomes will provide satisfaction at a personal level and if possible be aligned to their personal purpose. For us this is so important that we dedicate an entire chapter to it where we discuss the concept of purpose in more detail (see Chapter 11).

INVOLVEMENT

It is virtually impossible to be highly engaged without being involved. It's therefore essential that as a team leader, you are careful to involve and include all the members of your team. Research by Will Schutz for the US Naval Research Lab (Schutz, 1992, 1994) showed that inclusion and involvement is one of the fundamental psychological needs that humans have, although we vary as to how much inclusion we need. So, how do you go about involving and including your team members? Do you know how much inclusion they need or how much involvement they want?

It can be very easy as team leaders to fall into the habit of telling and giving direction and opinions, so involving others can be as simple as asking what their thoughts are *before* you tell them what yours are. American writer Stephen Covey said that one of the habits of effective leaders was 'Seek first to understand, then to be understood' (Covey, 2004). This is a good rule to apply in your teams whether you are a team leader or member.

We have two suggestions, the first one is for you to get into the habit of inquiring first before advocating your position. The second one is learning **NOT** to say 'Yes. . . . But!' What we are talking about here is when a team member makes a suggestion and you then say, 'I agree. . . BUT' and then go on to disagree. What we suggest you do instead is firstly look for what you might agree with in their statement, and then say for example, 'What I like about your idea is (then you insert a positive statement) **AND** we could also do (here you can insert your idea)'. In this way you are seeking to understand and building on your team member's idea rather than just dismissing it out of hand. In this way you are involving others and including them in the thinking process.

APPRECIATION

The need to be valued and appreciated is also a basic human need, and if you are to get successful performance from your team, then you need to be able to grasp the basic psychology of appreciation. We believe that team members have more energy and are more effective and creative when they enjoy their work, and one of the key mechanisms for this is to be valued and appreciated by their colleagues and their managers.

There are two simple steps to Appreciation, the first is **Noticing**. It's actually quite difficult to do this. We need to pay attention to what is going on around us, and then focus on what our team members are doing that is good (Positive reinforcement). We need to develop appreciative eyes and ears and an appreciative instinct. We need to both look for and listen for what is going well, without looking to judge, criticise or evaluate. We have to learn to ignore at times, the things we dislike and instead focus on what is positive. We also need to try to create a culture of appreciation within the team. Are our team members appreciative or critical in their own interactions?

The second is **Sharing**. It's not enough to just appreciate silently, we need to share it with the person or persons concerned. As a manager, leader or a team member, you might be thinking that the team get paid for doing good work and that should be enough, but you would be wrong.

What happens in this case is that no one values and appreciates what's going well, but it is very likely that what's not going well is noticed and criticised. So, the team never hears what is liked but always hear what isn't liked. This doesn't engage or energise people.

So to actively measure how engaged a team is, you might start by choosing one of the three perspectives above, or even better, create your own set of engagement behaviours within the team, drawing inspiration from these three perspectives.

TEAM LEADERS AND ENGAGEMENT

We know from research that many employees are disengaged and that the key factor in engagement is the direct manager (source – Macleod report). So, first of all what does an engaging manager do? Research from the UK's Institute of Employment Studies Research, as well as our own evidence from discussion with thousands of team members, tells us that an engaging team leader:

- communicates and makes clear what is expected from the team
- listens, values and involves teams
- is supportive and backs up their team
- is target focused
- shows empathy
- has a clear strategic vision
- shows active interest in others
- possesses good leadership skills
- is respected by the team
- is able to deal with poor performance and deliver bad news.

Ask yourself how your team leadership measures up to these criteria? You might want to use these criteria to rate yourself and ask your team to rate you on a scale of 1 to 10, with 10 being excellent. Then you can initiate an open and frank conversation with your team and listen to any suggested improvements you and the team could make.

What else can be done to create an engaging team? In our opinion there are a number of specific things that can done if you want to engage your team more effectively. We have broken the list into two parts – one which focuses on Interpersonal skills and the other which focuses on Processes:

Part 1 – Interpersonal skills

- **Autonomy and empowerment.** This is about building trust and involving your team members more.

- **Feedback, praise and recognition.** The effective team leader is able and skilled to give positive feedback and be appreciative (see more in Chapter 12).

- **Individual interest.** The level of genuine care and concern you have for your team members.

- **Personal manner.** The team leader demonstrates a positive approach and leads by example. It's about your manner and how positive and appreciative you are.

- **Reviewing and guiding.** The engaging team leader offers timely help and advice as and when necessary.

Part 2 – Processes

- **Development.** Providing time and opportunity for your team to develop and progress.

- **Availability.** The effective team leader holds regular one-to-one meetings and is available for the team and individual team members.

- **Ethics.** The engaging team leader shows fairness and respects confidentiality.

- **Clarifying expectations.** The engaging team leader sets clear goals and objectives and is willing to explain them. We often see team leaders doing the first part, but not all team leaders are so good at taking the time to explain the goals and objectives.

- **Managing time and resources.** The engaging team leader is fully aware of the team's workload and arranges for extra resources or redistributes work as and when necessary.

- **Following processes and procedures.** The engaging team leader understands, explains and follows all relevant work processes.

ENGAGING FEATURES REVIEW

Not all of these criteria will be relevant to your team; however, it's important to carry out an honest self-appraisal (perhaps with feedback from the team) as to how you measure up and be prepared to make any necessary changes to your behaviour.

Use the chart below to assess your own behaviour in each of these areas, score yourself out of 10 where 10 is excellent and then make notes about how you can further develop in each area. Before doing this, you may find it useful to explore how your team feel about their levels of engagement and why, perhaps asking for examples of what you do in terms of engaging them. This might provide you with some evidence of what you are doing or not doing well.

REFLECTION

Engaging Features Review		
Features	Score out of 10	Notes for development
Autonomy and empowerment		
Development		
Feedback, praise and recognition		
Individual interest		
Availability		
Personal manner		
Ethics		
Reviewing and guiding		
Clarifying expectations		
Managing time and resources		
Following processes and procedures		

Write down any general notes for improving engagement in my team

BARRIERS TO ENGAGEMENT

What gets in the way of engagement? We believe there are a range of barriers which prevent a high-level engagement. These include:

- a culture where no appreciation is shown
- the setting and imposing of unfair, unrealistic deadlines and objectives
- lack of respect between team members
- unfair and uneven treatment of team members
- a culture where there is a clear lack of listening.

Nigel has witnessed several examples of head coaches in high-level sports teams failing to engage with their teams effectively and losing their support. These can be summarised into five key points.

1. Lack of clarity concerning team purpose and strategy.
2. Losing team trust due to inconsistent selection/rotation and feedback.
3. Not living the team values (one rule for the leader another for the team).
4. Lack of appreciation of team and individual effort/commitment and not celebrating success.
5. Abdicating responsibility for poor results (blaming others).

We were reminded in an interview with Swedish clinical psychologist Hans Friberg of another barrier that detracts from team engagement. This is the concept of social loafing, which was first identified in 1913 by French Professor of Agricultural Engineering Max Ringelmann. Social loafing occurs when a person exerts less effort to achieve goals when working in a group than when working alone. Social loafing can occur unconsciously whenever there is a group of people working together. So, if we notice that others are seriously concentrating or focused on the issue, we might be tempted to contribute less thinking power to the problem, especially if we are tired or stressed. This also means that there is a danger of individuals hiding behind team decisions, especially if there is a lack of accountability within the team. The question then becomes, how do we track individual effort within the team? The best way is by ensuring that team members' performances are measured individually, and that the individual's performance is held to account as well as the team's performance.

It is important for team leaders from all walks of life to avoid these common traps and to seek regular open and honest feedback from their team.

WHOSE RESPONSIBILITY IS ENGAGEMENT?

There is a danger when it comes to engaging the team that all the responsibility ends up with the team leader, which leads to the team members themselves abdicating responsibility. What would then happen if the team leader isn't present? Dominic Mahoney, formerly a Captain in the British Army Lifeguard Regiment (the tank regiment), Olympic medallist and until recently team manager of the GB Olympic Modern Pentathlon team, tells us that too much can be made of the leader, and that the best teams have leadership 'on the field' as well (personal communication, 2018). Excellent teams have more leadership within themselves than we give credit for, and this is demonstrated in sport by winning teams such as the New Zealand All Blacks (with the highest winning percentage of any team) and Sir Clive Woodward's English Rugby World Cup winning team in 2003.

The All Blacks have established relay leaders on the field and their process hands leadership over fully to the players for the actual match itself. Many teams have moved to a more devolved model of 'on-field' leadership by appointing co-captains. There has been a significant shift in sport away from the single leadership model to a model where leadership can be seen at every level. The key is clarity of purpose, common goals and giving team members the permission to make decisions and to ultimately become more connected, responsible and accountable for the outcomes of their team.

These lessons from sports teams can be readily applied to other teams in organisations. In essence it means:

- don't micromanage
- make sure you have relay leaders (that is leaders among the team who can relay the team leader's perspective)
- be prepared to eventually hand leadership (as much as possible) over to the team itself.

MEASURING ENGAGEMENT

The most common way of measuring staff engagement seems to be organisation-wide surveys. The problem is that they tend to be somewhat blunt instruments and even if engagement is reported to be low, can (or will) the organisation do anything about it? We have all worked for organisations which have received less than perfect engagement scores on surveys but very little was actually done about it. This then just leads to even more disengagement with the process. If you are going to use an engagement survey you have to commit to making changes, otherwise don't bother. The main factor in engagement is the team leader (70 per cent according to studies) and the difficulty then becomes what system or training you put in place to help the managers and team leaders make changes to their behaviours.

It is our belief that a far more reliable measure of engagement would be where leaders at all levels in an organisation have staff engagement featured as one of their key objectives. Discussions about engagement should be encouraged and feature as a common part of any teams' regular meetings. Team members should be part of any discussions and involved in and responsible for ensuring engagement is present and identifying what engagement means for them. It is important to remember that engagement means different things to different people, so this is a fluid process that must be constantly worked on to ensure peak performance and commitment to the team and organisation.

Michelin-starred chef and restaurateur Tom Kerridge points out:

Attitude and willingness to learn is the biggest thing – you can mould that if people are willing to learn. So much of success comes from attitude. There are many many people in our company, within our group that work within our kitchens that haven't come from Michelin Star kitchens, they haven't come from top restaurants, they've come from places that have nothing to do with this environment. Aaron the Head Chef at the Hand of Flowers for 12 years came from Virgin Mobile! It was his attitude and enthusiasm to getting it right and learning that made him a success. Ollie Brown was a Sous Chef for us for a long time. For about 8 years before he joined us, he was working at John Lewis in the canteen. He came to help one Friday night because he wanted to work in a proper kitchen and see what it was like. He came back on the Saturday morning instead of going back to work at John Lewis. I told him I didn't have a job for him but, he said 'I don't care', and he kept coming back every day. We then had to pay him, and he stayed with us for 8 or 9 years. It was his attitude not his experience. Sometimes in sport you see players with great CVs but when you look at them their attitude isn't right; they don't fit in to the team. (Interview and personal communication with authors, 2021)

As Tom suggests, engagement is mostly about a person's attitude and willingness to learn, which are good reflectors of their ability to engage.

CHAPTER 9

BUILDING TRUSTING RELATIONSHIPS

'A team is not a group of people who work together.
A team is a group of people who trust each other.'

Simon Sinek (2009), *Start with Why: How great leaders inspire everyone to take action*. Portfolio.

INTRODUCTION

Trust between team members and within any team environment is a large part of what makes the difference between a bunch of individuals working together in service of their objectives, and an effective and high-performing team – in other words a team that works.

General Stanley McChrystal *et al.* in their book *Team of Teams* write about how the formation of United States Navy's elite SEAL teams is less about preparing people to follow precise orders and more about developing trust and the ability to adapt. Research also shows us that there is a higher return on shareholder investment, in firms where employees trust senior management (Hornstein, 2002).

Other studies tell us that trust in management is the most valued determinant of job satisfaction, and that people who trust each other work more effectively together – which is something that we all feel instinctively. But how much do people actually trust each other and their bosses? A survey of nearly 13,000 employees by Watson Wyatt indicated that fewer than two out of five employees trusted or had confidence in their leaders (Caudron, 2002). So, there is clearly room for improvement in levels of trust. Similarly, the 2016 PWC Global CEO survey reported that 55 per cent of CEOs think that a lack of trust is a threat to their organisation's growth.

We asked ex-rugby player Maggie Alphonsi MBE, who won the World Cup with England in 2014, how important trust was to a high-performing team.

> *Ah very very important ! Trust is so important and we underestimate it – when things are going well trust doesn't feel it needs to be so poignant and relevant but when things don't go well and you start to lose and you have to make some big decisions during a game and there are fine margins, trust is very important at that point because I have to trust you as a player, as a captain and I have to follow you – that's when trust becomes really important when the team isn't going as well as you want it to . So I felt that when I look at the England team that I was a part of between 2006 and 2014, I felt that trust built as time went on. They say that trust is like a dripping tap, it takes ages to build but when you break it it's like a flood. The team that won that World Cup spent a lot of time trying to develop that trust and our team psychologist helped with this.* (Private communication, 2022)

So, we can see that trust is essential for a team that works well, but it is a very intangible concept. What exactly do we mean when we say we trust someone? How is it created and how do you maintain trust within teams? This chapter will define what we mean by trust and will illustrate ways of creating, building, developing, maintaining and deepening trust within team environments.

IMPACT OF LACK OF TRUST

If there is a lack of trust then the team will not be honest with each other, team members will not confide in each other and will not be able to rely on each other. The team will not then be as effective as it could or should be. You could say that trust is at the heart of the team. Without trust, the word team is basically redundant. As Simon Sinek implied, without trust you are simply a group of people working together (Sinek, 2011).

In high-level sports teams for example, Nigel has found that trust is extremely important. As an example, team members will be asking themselves the following questions about their colleagues just before a game:

- Can we trust you to do your job when the time comes?
- Can we trust that you to have prepared well for the game?
- Can we trust that you will give everything for this team?

Teams are interdependent entities; everyone has their position or role to play. If you cannot trust a colleague to do their job you will have to cover for them and this will then have the negative effect of taking your focus away from your own role, and thus reducing performance. Newly formed teams are asking those questions for the first time, but they don't yet know to what degree they can trust their fellow team members. Highly effective teams – teams that work – don't need to ask those questions – they know their team will be ready because they have *already* worked on establishing trust. High trust levels are therefore an important part of high-performing teams.

We spoke to Sir Andrew Strauss, one of England's best ever cricketers and former England cricket captain and asked him if he thought trust was important. This is what he said:

Ultimately no team environment works without trust. Trust is the foundation, if you don't trust those around you, ... if you don't feel like you can be honest and open and say how you really feel then actually it's a non-functioning team. You need to know in that team that everyone has your best interests at heart. If you suspect or know that other people in that team are untrustworthy in that regard, i.e., they are putting their own interests ahead of those of the team and they don't believe in what you are trying to do, then you are gone before you even start. So, that trust element is crucially important, and by the way, it's a lot easier said than done to get to that level, if you bear in mind that international sport is quite transient with new players coming and going and old players retiring. (Personal interview with authors, 2021)

As Sir Andrew suggests, you cannot rest on your laurels with trust as teams and organisations are always changing and evolving too.

REFLECTION

Think about the team you spend most of your time in. Make a list of all the team members including the leader. Using your own natural instincts rate each person using a scale of 1 being low level to 5 being absolute trust. Now make notes about why you rate each person this way. Keep this list safe as you may like to revisit it later in the chapter.

WHAT DO WE MEAN BY TRUST?

We've established that trust is a critical factor for teams that work, but for you to establish trust in your team, you need to have a more specific idea of what exactly trust involves, how to measure it and how much trust you need in the team. We often hear people saying, 'I trust you', but how can you trust someone without first defining what you mean by trust? It's pretty much meaningless to just say, 'I trust you'. You have to be specific and say something like 'I trust you to do x or y'. We often think of trust as a value which we hold, but it actually needs to be built by specific behaviours, so it's not enough to announce that you can be trusted – you have to demonstrate through specific behaviours over time that you can actually be trusted. There are several different ways of looking at trust. An insightful way of looking at some of the specific behaviours of building trust is given by Dennis and Michelle Reina in their book, *Trust and Betrayal in the Workplace* (2015). They write about three specific types of trust and we have adapted their ideas. The model below illustrates our approach.

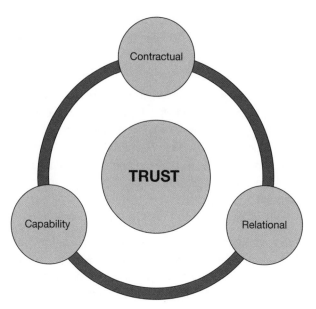

Adapted from Reina, D. and Reina, M. *Trust and betrayal at work*

CAPABILITY TRUST

This is where we trust in people's capabilities to do something. In sports terms, if a teammate passes the ball to you, will you be able to catch it? Or, to give a business example, if I ask you to run a seminar for me, do you actually have the competence to run and deliver it successfully?

> ### EXAMPLE
>
> *When Nigel coached the Gloucester Rugby team (who play in the Premiership in England) they developed a very strong and effective defensive system, but the defensive line is only as strong as its weakest link. The system was a human chain, where every player was a link. Each player had to keep the line connected and trust that the player on their inside would make their tackle, so that they could focus on making their own tackle. If any player didn't trust the player on their inside to make that tackle, they would hesitate and wait for their teammate to make the tackle, before focusing on their own tackle. That lack of trust leads to vital seconds being lost and could put a player out of position to make their own tackle. So, trust plays a critical role in creating an effective defence and not breaking the chain. Each player needed to trust that their colleague had the competency to make the tackle and that they would make it!*

It's the same in organisations – if you don't trust the competency of a colleague, then you can't focus 100 per cent on the job you need to do!

BUILDING CAPABILITY TRUST

Building trust takes time so you have to be prepared to invest time and effort in doing it. Michelin-starred chef Tom Kerridge is clear that fear is a blocker to creativity, engagement and performance. Tom owns the exceptional Hand and Flowers pub in Marlow in England – the only two-starred Michelin public house in the UK (2021) – and also runs a business which includes four restaurants, a butchers, an event business and a festival business, with around 200 employees.

Tom Kerridge explains how he builds trust in his kitchen.

Young guys start with the little jobs, well the least expensive jobs in case they muck up and they are more likely to muck up as they don't have the experience. They need to learn to respect potatoes and broccoli because if they muck up potatoes and broccoli it's not the same cost implications as it is if they are learning about sea bass and beef fillets. By the time you get to cooking sea bass and beef fillets you have a good understanding of how kitchens work. (Private communication with authors)

Tom is not going to let a young, untrained person loose on expensive cuts of meat or fish. The young chef has to start with the vegetables and prove that they can respect these and cook them properly. Once they have proved this, then, and only then, will they be trusted to work with meat and vegetables. '*As they get better, they will be given greater responsibility, but they have to learn to respect potatoes and broccoli as much as they would sea bass or beef fillets.*'

What are the equivalents of potatoes and broccoli in your team?

CONTRACTUAL TRUST

This is where we place our trust in people's characters ... and we trust them to respect agreements and keep promises. This is clearly an essential part of effective teamwork, because if this type of trust is broken then the team cannot perform effectively. If you make a promise and don't keep it, then your trust account goes back down to zero. You don't just lose the trust of the individual but of all the team members, as you can be sure that news of your broken promise will spread throughout the team.

In individual sports like tennis or golf, a player walks onto the court or course knowing exactly how well they have prepared for competition.

But in business and sports teams we have to trust that our colleagues have also done everything they could do to prepare for the project or game. Successful teams have a high degree of trust that everyone has prepared well. Actions speak louder than words when building contractual trust; colleagues and teammates will be watching how you prepare and perform, and trust will be developed over time.

EXAMPLE

In sport an important form of contractual trust is team selection. The players trust that the coach will select the team based on the criteria they have set for the team. That selection will be based on performance and not influenced by relationships or favouritism. Individually the players want to trust their coach to be 'fair and transparent'; this form of trust can break down very easily and can negatively impact the development of the team.

REFLECTION

You might like to ask yourself how you measure contractual trust in your team. For instance, do you make explicit contracts with each other about what you can expect in terms of behaviour and performance? Or is it just **assumed** that you trust each other?

RELATIONAL TRUST

This is where we trust people not to disclose secrets, to respect confidences, to tell the truth and to generally respect each other. This type of trust is vital to ensure an effective team. Effective team performance relies on each person telling the truth, but if your colleague thinks you'll repeat to others what they said to you about their concerns or anxieties about a project for example, then they simply will not confide in you. Then what happens is that no one is sharing their concerns with anyone and there is no opportunity for these concerns to be addressed.

As Sir Andrew Strauss said, *'If you don't feel like you can be honest and open and say how you really feel then actually it's a non-functioning team'.*

REFLECTION

How is relational trust established, built and developed in your team? How would you rate your teammates and team leader on relational trust? You can do this by asking each person to rate trust on a scale of 1 to 10 (10 being highest). If for example the average was 6 you could begin by asking – what brought it up to a 6? In other words what are we doing well? Then you might explore what else you could do to score even higher.

Clearly we need all three types of trust within teams, and we need to be specific about the type of trust and the degree of trust. If we use the three types of trust, we can start to narrow down the specific types of trust we are talking about. For example, I might fully trust my colleague to tell the truth – and to keep their promises – *relational trust* – but still not trust them to do their job properly – *capability trust*.

For us trust is another one of the processes that need to be discussed upfront in the early stages of a team's creation. It should also form part of the regular discussions you have with your team both when you meet as a team and when you meet one to one. One possibility is to develop regular feedback processes to help build trust. See Chapter 12.

You need to decide which of these three types of trust are the most important for your team, and which of them you need from team members in each situation. Is one type of trust more important in a particular team situation or do you need to move towards developing all three levels of trust?

THE TRUST EQUATION

Another interesting way you can measure trust is by using the Trust Equation developed by David Maister and his colleagues (2002). This looks at different factors involved in building Trust – which are Credibility, Reliability, Intimacy and the degree of Self-orientation people have.

They created an equation to illustrate what they believed trust to be:

$$\text{Trust} = \frac{\text{Credibility} + \text{Reliability} + \text{Intimacy}}{\text{Self-Orientation}}$$

This is a great starting point for understanding what trust means between individuals in your team. Maister and his colleagues suggested that trust is a combination of elements which all operate together to create an environment where team members have developed high-quality connections and relationships with each other.

Credibility is about an individual's impact. Is their behaviour consistent and do they have the knowledge, skills and expertise that they claim to have? In essence, do their actions give others a feeling of authenticity and genuineness? Are they really who they say they are in terms of delivery and performance? The higher the person's credibility, the more likely they are to be trustworthy.

In your team you have to reflect on how you build your credibility in any given situation or context. That involves an open conversation about expectations among team members:

- What do I expect from you?
- What do you expect from me?
- How do we meet these expectations?

Credibility, like respect, is hard won and easily lost. In team sports, an individual's capabilities are usually well documented in the media – we know what they are capable of. We know what they have achieved, where they have played and with who. However, integrity matters too.

Reliability is about how dependable you are. Can you be counted upon to deliver your promises? To turn up on time. To do what you said you were going to do? If you make a promise, then break that promise, clearly other members of your team will be unlikely to believe any of your future promises. They probably aren't going to call you a liar to your face, but you will gradually notice that you won't be included in interesting work. Also, your colleagues will respect you less. It's even worse if you are the team leader. If you are not seen as reliable, then the whole team suffers and performance will drop rapidly. In sport, people talk about players being a 'great professional'. These are the reliable ones: the ones who are not necessarily the most gifted, but put in the extra hours on the training field. They are on time, wear the right kit, look after themselves, always give 100 per cent, put the team first and are fantastic ambassadors for the team.

Intimacy is about your ability to build, develop and maintain relationships with others. Clearly, effective teamwork is built on effective relationships between the team leader and his or her team members and between the team members themselves.

The best teams are like families, they don't have to be best friends, but they share a common purpose and recognise the value each brings to the team. Sports teams spend a lot of time together, including time training, then traveling to games, staying in hotels, waiting for the kickoff on game days, and then only a relatively short time in actually performing. It's an emotional roller coaster over a long season, based on wins and losses. Intra-team relationships are therefore critical to the success of any team. Winning sports teams create a flow, a momentum during the season. They learn to respect others' space and feelings, they celebrate success together and stay close when performances dip. Managing the intimacy of the team is critical to success and an important part of team leadership for captains and coaches, managers and support staff.

REFLECTION

How good are the relationships in your team? How could you create a similar intimacy in your team? What could help develop intimacy and effective relationships in your team context?

Self-orientation is where individuals are focused only on their own needs rather than with other team members as well. Clearly, too much self-orientation will detract from trust. In fact, self-oriented people will find it almost impossible to establish long-lasting trusting relationships with others, as they are more concerned with their own well-being than with the well-being of the team as a whole. High self-orientation is the antithesis of effective teamwork. The idea here is to have the lowest possible score – in other words a low *self*-orientation and therefore a high *other* orientation.

REFLECTION

How to use the trust equation

The idea of the trust equation is that you can use it as a catalyst to have conversations about Trust within your team rather than just scoring each other. You can take each of the first three criteria and score them out of 10 (10 being the highest and 1 the lowest). Of course these scores will change for each different role you play.

How credible am I?

How reliable am I?

How well do I know my team members? (and how well do they know me?) We would recommend that team members score themselves and then have a discussion with their colleagues rather than having the whole team score each other. So, not everyone has to have a 10 on the top line or a 1 on the self-orientation score. Maybe a 6 is good enough on intimacy for your team. You would then discuss what that actually looked like in terms of what you reveal to others or what others want to know about you.

How do you believe others would rate you on the trust criteria?

Credibility	• 1 2 3 4 5 6 7 8 9 10
Reliability	• 1 2 3 4 5 6 7 8 9 10
Intimacy	• 1 2 3 4 5 6 7 8 9 10
Self Orientation	• 1 2 3 4 5 6 7 8 9 10

Once you have scored this table, use it to have a conversation with your colleagues about how you can develop more trust in your relationships.

Trust is a difficult concept to measure and often people talk about the general feeling they have about others – sometimes referred to as their 'gut reaction'. If you apply the characteristics explained above and recognise that self-orientation will detract from trust within any relationship, then you will be beginning the process of building trust with others.

CREATING AND MAINTAINING THE CULTURE OF TRUST IN A TEAM

KEY THINGS YOU CAN DO TO INCREASE TRUST IN YOUR TEAM

We believe that there are nine key things that you can do to increase trust in your team or organisation, and these can be implemented very easily. Elements of each of these ideas can be used no matter whether your team is coming together for a short-term project, a virtual team or a long-term project team.

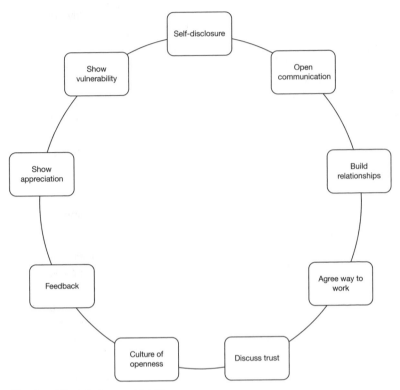

Nine key things to increase trust

Let's examine each of these areas.

Use self-disclosure

Firstly, as a team leader open up to others and tell the team a bit about the real you – not just the work-based stuff! Tell people about your hobbies and interests, the things that make you feel good and the things that upset you. The important thing here is to be genuine and let your team get to know a bit more about you. This will model the way for team members to feel more comfortable about opening up and sharing more of their real selves.

Create regular open communication

Make sure that you share information with the team in a timely and appropriate manner. One of the things that creates a barrier to building trust is when the people in a team hear information 'through the grapevine' or through a third party rather than from their boss. Have regular face-to-face meetings, and also have other methods of communication established so that you can get information to people quickly and easily. Once you have shared information with the team, ensure you create the opportunity for all team members to share, explore and discuss, to ensure they understand what it means and what the implications for the individuals and the team might be.

For example, at leading UK management consultancy, Lane 4, anybody in the company can have access to the monthly figures. This clearly shows trust in the organisation's people and of course, you can have a clear acceptance that the information stays within the company. So be as open and upfront about information as you can be.

Get to know each other personally and build relationships

We have found that teams that engender trust and perform well together will tend to have a far more in-depth knowledge of one another. Taking time to organise team away days, team lunches or other team events will enable you to begin this process.

You can borrow something from high-performance sports teams and take a moment after a busy session to review the performance of the team, including the levels of trust, and what you all need personally from the others in order to trust your team mates even more. For example, in a sales team, that moment might be right after a busy pitch. You've all worked 12 hours a day for 7 days including the weekend and delivered a great pitch to your client right on time. But it's important not to rush on to the next pitch immediately, and you need to take some time to debrief what went well and what didn't, but specifically asking about the levels and types of trust within the team.

It can take time to get to know each other as some individuals are naturally more reticent than others, but if you model self-disclosure, then very often team members will find it easier to follow suit. At meetings or other team events, encourage people to share some personal informa-tion about themselves. Don't rush people though, let them develop team relationships at their own pace. For example, when we start off seminars, we ask people to share the usual stuff – like who you are, where you're from and what you do. But we also ask them to share something different about themselves. One of our favourite questions is 'Tell us something that a lot of people don't know about you'. Participants then tell us about interesting hobbies, embarrassing but funny moments in their life and all sorts of stories. This then opens up something personal and breaks down barriers really quickly.

Work together to agree ways of working in the team

We find that teams who spend time thinking about how they will work together, and actually create their own rules and processes are more committed and trusting of one another. In this area much will depend upon the purpose of the team, but some possibilities for discussions about how to work together are:

- Talk about the team values – what is it that each team member values about working as part of this team?
- Talk about the behaviours that team members would find acceptable and unacceptable within the team.
- Create a team charter/mission statement which codifies the way you want to work together.

Team charters take many different forms, some are boldly displayed on the team room wall signed by all the team as a show of commitment to the team, others end up in a desk drawer and never see the light of day.

Nigel believes that a commitment to a team purpose (see Chapter 11) that becomes a bit of a mantra for the team (one they can remember and rally behind) is a powerful way to unite the team. When Nigel was Chief Executive of USA Rugby, the staff and board used the phrase 'Inspire Americans to Fall in Love with Rugby', as an elevator pitch that could be used on a daily basis. Underpinning the purpose are team rules but be careful not to rely too much on rules as illustrated in the example below.

Nigel recalls:

At Wasps (the English premiership rugby club) we had rules and a system of fines, which was important and set the boundaries for the team. However, the list of rules started to grow and grow, and the more rules you have, the more rules are broken, and before too long I was dealing with a weekly list of rule breakers and fines. I became the police, judge and jury, and that did not help my relationship with the players, some who were being fined by me on a weekly basis!

When I moved to Gloucester rugby Club (another English premiership team) I created a much simpler system based on what were the 'redlines' for me getting the best from the team each week. They were.

1. Right Place (as in be where you need to be)

2. Right Time (do not be late)

3. Right Kit (wearing whatever you should be wearing)

4. Right Attitude (a positive attitude and ready to work)

These 'redlines' simplified things and worked extremely well, and I also created a fines committee to manage the process!

Discuss what kind of trust and how much trust you need to have in the team

In some teams a lack of trust is literally a matter of life and death, in others it might mean losing the game, while in others it might be a question of damaging relationships or preventing optimal work. You don't need 100 per cent trust in everyone in every situation. What you do need is to have conversations about what kind of trust you need in your team generally and then in each specific situation. The English psychologist Donald Winnicott created the term 'good enough' in respect of parenting. He reminded mothers that there was no such thing as the perfect parent, and he suggested that they put all their attention on their child at first, but then gradually focus less on the child and allow the child to become more independent (Winnicott, 1971). We feel it's somewhat similar with trust in the team. There is no perfect degree of trust, but there needs to be 'good enough' trust for the team to perform effectively. It's up to the team, with the help of the team leader, to decide what exactly 'good enough' trust looks like. So, go ahead and openly discuss what kind of trust you need and how much and what that specifically looks like.

Create a culture of openness and encourage debate

This means that teams need to be able to debate issues in an open and honest way. One indicator of trust within a team is when team members feel that they can challenge, question and generally debate openly when working together. One of the main benefits of working in a team is that you have the opportunity to share and hear many different perspectives. If trust is low, then team members will not speak up or tell the truth as they see it. Creating the environment for high-quality debate will enable you to build trust and openness, which leads to better quality outcomes overall. High-trust organisations get better results. (See Chapter 4 on Psychological Safety.)

Create a culture of feedback and feedforward

Another good method of building openness and trust is to develop an environment where feedback between all team members is welcome and common. There are many different ways of doing this. Here are some ideas:

- Just before the end of a team meeting ask each person to turn to the person next to them and say one thing they appreciated about working with them during the meeting or in the team in general. At the next meeting use a similar process but this time ask them to give one piece of positive feedback and also one piece of developmental feedback. This sort of feedback can then be built into the regular team meeting process.

- Create a full 360-degree feedback process between all team members. In order to get more thoughtful and meaningful data, ask team members to write down feedback for each member of the team (including the leader). It is best to use a process here whereby individuals answer three questions – for instance:

  o What should this individual continue doing as part of their team contribution?

  o What should this individual stop doing?

  o What should this individual do to further develop their contribution to the team?

- Or the questions could be as simple as:

  o Stop?

  o Start?

  o Continue?

The overall idea here is that team members share their experiences of each other as part of a developmental and trust building process. A further refinement of this process is one used by several blue-chip international companies. The individuals are asked to create their own criteria for feedback and then these criteria are given to selected (by the participant themselves) feedback givers. The feedback givers then give their ratings on these criteria and these are then pulled together by an external coach, who gives the feedback to the participant. This then becomes a bespoke 360-degree feedback process.

For these ideas to be successful and for trust to be developed and maintained as part of the team's way of working you must commit to operating and behaving in an authentic way. These ideas are not simply one-off techniques: each one of them must be built into the team's way of working for them to have long-lasting and meaningful results.

Be appreciative and recognise good work

We are usually very good at recognising what's going wrong with an individual's performance within the team. But we're less good at noticing when people are doing things right. We are much more likely to create motivation and engagement when we start to notice what people are doing well. The need to be valued and appreciated is a basic human need and it's important for team leaders and team members to be able to show appreciation. There are two simple steps to appreciating – Noticing and Sharing.

- **Noticing.** This means developing an appreciative instinct, to look for and listen for what is going well. You have to learn to ignore at times the things you dislike and instead focus on the positives. You also need to create this positive atmosphere within the team itself and create a culture of appreciation within the team. This doesn't mean that you can't ever give critical feedback, but it does mean that you must also give feedback when things are going well.

- **Sharing.** It's not enough just to notice what people are doing well – you have to actually tell them. As a team leader you might think that your team get paid for doing things well and that this is enough. But then team members never hear what you value about them or what their strengths are but have a very clear idea of what you don't like! This is extremely demotivating. As a rule of thumb, we'd suggest giving four positive pieces of feedback to one negative one. Of course, that means sometimes NOT telling someone all the things they've done wrong AND focusing more on what they are doing well.

Show vulnerability

No one is perfect and it's counterproductive to pretend that anyone is. We all have strengths and weaknesses, and it helps to create trust if we can be more open and honest about these. You may think you are perfect, but you can be sure that your flaws are obvious and visible to those around you. Research by London Business School professors Rob Goffee and Gareth Jones shows that effective leaders selectively share their weaknesses, and by expressing some vulnerability they reveal their approachability and humanity (Goffee and Jones, 2019). This also creates more trust as it gives team members the space to reveal their own weaknesses.

Adrian Moorhouse, Olympic gold medallist, and now Managing Partner EY/Lane 4, describes when he was working with leaders involved in a major retail organisational merger. He felt that the most effective and productive sessions were the ones where the leaders of the company were open and admitted to being a bit scared about the merger. For Adrian it is important that he has to be able to say what he feels, and that this applies to the whole company – that everyone at Lane 4 should be able to say what they feel openly.

REFLECTION

Questions

Think of a team which you belong or belonged to which had high elements of trust. Why was this?

How did this trust impact the performance team?

Complete the table below. Rate each component on a scale of 1 to 7. With 1 being lowest and 7 highest. Once you have completed it you can ask your team members to complete it too. The idea is to see the spread of answers and use them to have open conversations about where the team is and what it needs to do in order to increase trust within the team.

	1 Low	2	3	4	5	6	7 High
Self-disclosure							
Regular open communication							
Know each other							
Agreed ways of working							
Discuss what kind of trust and how much trust							
Openness							
Culture of feedback							
Appreciation							
Reveal vulnerability							

CHAPTER 10

DEALING WITH CONFLICT EFFECTIVELY

'Dialogue is the most effective way of resolving conflict.'

Tenzin Gyatso, The 14th Dalai Lama

INTRODUCTION

Conflict and confrontation are facts of life. When people work together there are bound to be differences. For instance: difference of opinion, difference in personality, difference in skills and difference in experience, as well as the more obvious differences of age, gender and nationality – any of these differences can cause conflict to arise. We believe that conflict, when handled effectively, can be productive and is often a key feature in high-performance teams. The challenge is how the various people involved, the team leader as well as the team members, deal with the conflict. It is important to recognise and distinguish between healthy, productive conflict and unhealthy. dysfunctional conflict.

Writer Patrick Lencioni observes that the ability to have productive conflict is one of the key building blocks of a high-performing team (Lencioni, 2002). If there are little or no conflicting views in the team, then that suggests that ideas are not being fully discussed, or that team members are not being fully open and honest or that the team leader does not allow healthy debate within the team.

In any team situation there are a multitude of possibilities for where, when and with whom conflict can arise. As an example, within a team of say 6 people there are 30 possible inter-relationships all of which have the potential for generating conflict. Teams can also experience inter-team conflict, conflict with the organisation or certain people within the organisation and conflict can also arise with external stakeholders – customers, clients, suppliers.

Whatever the situation, whatever the cause and whoever is involved, it is important for leaders and their teams to be able to recognise when conflict exists, to have the skills to understand the nature of the conflict and to have the ability to resolve the conflict. Too many people in business turn a blind eye to conflict in the hope that it will go away. This is rarely the answer as dysfunctional conflict seldom solves itself. If left to incubate, conflict tends to escalate into a much bigger issue than if it had been dealt with promptly and effectively in the early stages when first identified or observed. Our experience with high-performance teams confirms that it is unwise to allow conflict to fester as things will only get worse if the conflict is not addressed.

We asked England International rugby player and World Cup winner Maggie Alphonsi about how the England womens' rugby team dealt with conflict and she told us that in the team they worked hard to develop '*good conflict*'.

She went on to explain that this meant that if she did something wrong then someone would call her out, but do it in a professional way, in a safe space.

This was also linked to the levels of trust within the team. If there was high trust then she felt she was not being called out as the other team member had some personal issue with her but because it was helpful to the team's overall objective. Maggie explained that the difference between the team of 2010 and that of the World Cup winning team in 2014 was that they were trying to create 'good conflict' and challenging each other, but doing it from a trusting and safe space. It wasn't personal.

In this chapter we will explore specific issues about conflict in teams, the difference between productive and dysfunctional conflict, symptoms and signs of conflict, and then move on to offering strategies and processes for coping with and resolving conflict.

HEALTHY VS. UNHEALTHY CONFLICT

When we ask team members about conflict, people immediately think about situations where the behaviours of those involved have been dysfunctional and unproductive, and the outcome has been negative, whether in relation to work output or relationships. However, conflict can be productive as it can encourage discussion, debate and creativity. One example of what can be regarded as healthy conflict is where team members disagree about ideas for developing a new process for greater efficiency at work. This sort of disagreement (or conflict of ideas) can lead to improvement in the outcome when all parties involved share their ideas and then move forward in service of the overall goal.

Of course, this requires the leader and the team to have a clear goal to work towards and then to be able to adopt a process that enables all parties involved to share their ideas and to explore the best possible outcomes. It sounds easy but it does require you to have in place good principles and processes for resolving conflict. This is essential if you want to have a team that works well.

So how do you recognise healthy and unhealthy conflict?

The chart that follows suggests some of the cues and clues we have observed.

Healthy Conflict tends to involve	Unhealthy Conflict tends to involve
■ Task focused issues	■ Personal attacks
■ Respectful debate exploring identified problems	■ Blaming others
■ Genuine differences of opinion	■ Anger and frustration being expressed
■ Differing values or perspectives on an issue	■ Manipulative or patronising behaviour
■ Win/Win mindset	■ Win/lose situations

The first thing you need to do when dealing with perceived conflict is to determine whether or not it might be healthy or unhealthy conflict. It often falls to the team leader to either help people work through the issue if the conflict is a healthy one, or alternatively to help resolve the issue if it is an unhealthy conflict. We will offer a process to follow later in this chapter.

SYMPTOMS AND SIGNS OF POTENTIAL CONFLICT

Recognising the symptoms and signs of conflict can help you to diagnose and deal with conflict early. The visible signs of conflict – personality clashes, anger, arguments between people, development of win/lose situations – are relatively easy to notice. It is the less obvious symptoms and signs that you must be aware of. It may be that you observe or sense some changes in the normal behaviour or way of working within your team. Picking up on these symptoms and signs can be challenging, as they can be very subtle and will require you to be familiar with what's normal for the team and for the individuals within the team.

As a starting point, you may find it useful to reflect on your own behaviour when in conflict and what it is that causes you to move into your conflict zone.

REFLECTION

Reflect back over the past few weeks/months and identify a time when you have been in a conflict situation at work. Can you identify what it was that created the conflict? Think about the specific situation:

- Who was involved?
- What was said?
- How did you feel?
- What did you think?
- How did you respond?
- What specifically pushed you to feel in conflict?

By understanding your own behaviour when in conflict and being more self-aware of the changes in your own conduct, you can better appreciate the changes that others go through. The important issue here is for you to recognise that behavioural changes can be an indicator of people moving from their comfort zone into conflict.

One theory that we find very useful to help people understand what tips them into conflict is 'Relationship Awareness Theory', which was developed by Dr Elias H Porter (Porter, 1950). Part of his theory suggests that conflict happens when something important to you is threatened, and this then compromises your self-worth. This is often related to the values you hold, and of course this can be different for different people. When we have in-depth conversations with managers and leaders about conflict, we have found that very often they identify the following issues that act as their trigger.

■ Their competence being challenged.

■ Others being patronising, dismissive or aggressive towards them.

■ Their rights as an individual being challenged.

■ Someone being personally hostile.

■ Overly emotional behaviour by others.

■ A sense of being exploited by someone.

■ Having to deal with difficult people who have intractable personalities.

■ A feeling of being ignored.

Any of these feelings, if not recognised, can result in escalation towards conflict. The other interesting part of Porter's theory is that people do not usually move straight from *effective* behaviour to *conflict* behaviour. He suggests that we tend to go through a process of moving from effective behaviour to dysfunctional behaviour over a period of time. This time period can be very short with changes happening rapidly, or it can happen over a very long period. If you want to know more about this theory and how it works in practice you may find it useful to complete the Strength Deployment Inventory, which is the questionnaire Porter developed based on his theories. Information can be found at www.personalstrengths.uk.

Recognising the symptoms and signs of conflict can in some cases be easy. For instance, loud arguments between team members, when you are cc'd into irate emails from team members or other stakeholders, maybe at a team meeting when colleagues become entrenched, rivalry between teams that becomes unhealthy or even when you are dealing with a poor performer who has difficulty accepting your feedback. These are just a sample of the sorts of indicators that you might observe. Some visible signs of conflict are obvious, for instance, increased absences and sick leave. However, other indicators of conflict or potential conflict may not be so obvious.

- Observable subtle changes in behaviour within the team:
  - less general chit chat
  - increased periods of silence
  - some team members not engaging with others

- A general feeling of poor morale in the team
- Team members' levels of motivation dropping

EXAMPLE

CONFLICT BEING TRIGGERED

This example was shared with us during a discussion with a colleague. (We have changed the names to ensure confidentiality.)

Suzanne was a member of a team of management consultants who tended to work independently and only came together occasionally for team reviews. It was at one of these events that the conflict happened. She explained to us that she knew she had a short fuse towards a couple of her colleagues in the team based on her previous experience of their behaviour at such meetings. That behaviour was cynicism, patronising behaviour towards others and general lack of respect for other team members. She felt these people only attended such meetings to stir things up.

On this occasion Suzanne was sitting with a couple of her colleagues chatting when Jim arrived in the room and made a beeline for her group and sat down. His opening remarks on joining them were, 'Well here we are again. Another complete waste of a day'. Suzanne immediately snapped. She said to Jim, 'If that's how you feel then why on earth stay? Why not just go now and save us all a lot of grief having to put up with your whining and cynicism'. Jim then got up and walked out!

Suzanne went on to explain that she felt terrible afterwards, as she hadn't meant for this to happen. She simply wanted Jim to realise that his behaviour wasn't helpful. She did, however, realise that her reaction had been aggressive and confrontational. During our discussion we went on to explore her reaction and she realised that lack of respect shown to others was a major conflict trigger for her.

This type of conflict is quick and usually ends in a relationship breakdown – which in fact it did in this instance. Suzanne also explained that she was surprised by her own response in this particular situation and the speed of her reaction and anger. Her lesson from this experience was to try to control her short fuse and to think more deeply about the potential consequences of her remarks.

What might have been better in this scenario? When Jim started complaining about wasting his time, instead of snapping back at him Suzanne could have asked an open question and said something like, 'What makes you think the day will be wasted Jim?'. She could have then listened to Jim's explanation and empathised with it without necessarily agreeing with him. This would probably have helped Jim to calm down and share some of what was going through his head. As it was, he felt that Suzanne was attacking him, reacted emotionally and walked out of the meeting. This of course led to a worsening of the relationship between Suzanne and Jim but also between them and the rest of the team. They felt that Suzanne had been unskilful and Jim over emotional and lacking self-control.

We believe that as a team leader your ability to deal with conflict will be assisted by:

- keen observation skills
- good knowledge of your team members' usual behavioural patterns and motivations at work
- recognising changes and dealing with things early
- adopting a conflict resolution process that works for you.

What follows is a process that we have found useful in our work as coaches and consultants and also when managing our own teams.

CONFLICT RESOLUTION PROCESS

We offer the following seven-step process which can be used by anyone who takes on the role of conflict mediation. It encompasses the range of steps and stages necessary to diagnose whether or not the conflict is healthy or unhealthy and then a process to follow towards resolution. The very nature of conflict suggests that things are not flowing smoothly and therefore you may find that in using this process you have to flex it to suit the particular situation and people involved.

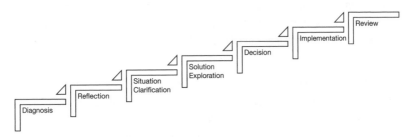

Conflict resolution process

Each of the stages in this process involves a range of skills, techniques and practices that can be used as described or adapted to suit your own situation.

Step 1 – Diagnosis. At this stage you have become aware that some disagreement, confrontation or other unusual behaviour is present within the team. The challenge here is to determine the extent of the disagreement, and whether or not it is simply a healthy debate or rather something that is escalating towards full-blown conflict. Observation is key at this stage. Be clear about what you are seeing, thinking and feeling that suggests there may be a conflict brewing. Focus on the issue and the people involved and establish how the situation arose by talking with all involved to identify the key issues.

Step 2 – Reflection. This is the stage where you must decide whether or not this is a case of healthy debate that you just need to keep an eye on. If you feel it is simply a healthy debate between co-workers, then your knowledge of the people involved and how they generally cope with debate and disagreement will be helpful. In addition to this, the topic of the disagreement may also have some bearing, for instance, the degree of freedom the people involved have to reach their own outcomes. You may need to facilitate the process to help the disagreement to reach a healthy outcome or alternatively to move towards conflict resolution.

If, on reflection, you feel the situation is building towards, or is already an unhealthy conflict, then you must intervene to ensure the issue reaches a satisfactory outcome. It is important that all the involved parties understand that your primary role is to help them resolve the issue and move on. If this is the case, agree with all involved where and when you will meet to begin the conflict resolution process. You might also indicate how you intend to progress, and that each person should be willing to talk about what's going wrong and come up with ideas for resolution in a professional manner. Your role here is to work with them to resolve the issue. not to tell them what to do.

Step 3 – Situation clarification. In this step questioning, listening, testing understanding and clarifying are the key skills. Your role now is to be sure that you have a clear understanding of the conflict issue from the perspective of all the parties involved and without judgement. In essence (and assuming you are not involved in the conflict process yourself) your role as a mediator is to encourage those involved in the conflict to describe the situation as they see it. You should encourage open dialogue (face to face if possible) where each person involved explains their perspective, their thoughts and feelings about the issue and any ideas they have for moving forward. The important thing now is to encourage and enable those involved to talk openly about the conflict issue, and for you to listen and understand so that you can help them towards a resolution that is acceptable for everyone.

Step 4 – Solution exploration. Once both you and those involved in the conflict feel that you have a clear understanding of the situation from all perspectives, it is time to explore possible solutions or ways ahead. Sometimes you may find that during the previous stage you have begun to develop possible solutions and you may like to begin with these. Then, if necessary, brainstorm with others to help you further develop a range of options and possibilities. Your role here is to help to create ideas, to enable movement by all involved, towards a mutually acceptable outcome.

Step 5 – Decision. Assuming you have effectively worked through the previous stages, all those involved should be beginning to appreciate each other's differing perspectives on the issue and that the best way ahead is to move towards a mutually acceptable outcome. This should be something that everyone can accept and live with and will often involve some degree of compromise. This stage should not be rushed, as it is vital to ensure that everyone understands the outcome. The important skills at this stage are clarity of language (to restate the decision), listening, clarification and summarising. Make sure everyone involved has verbally agreed (and in writing if necessary) the outcome and that they understand the mutual benefits of what has been agreed. Failure to get this stage right can lead to a re-ignition of the conflict.

Step 6 – Implementation. Your role now is to observe the implementation process. This is the time when you must assess whether or not the conflict resolution process has been successful or not, by observing how the solution works in practice. So your skills of listening and observing are important to gauge if the people involved are willing to work together to ensure success.

Step 7 – Review. Dealing with any conflict resolution process is not easy. Conflict almost always involves compromise and concessions and will be an emotional experience for all. However, it can also be a good learning opportunity. It is worth therefore reviewing the process to understand what worked, what didn't work and how you can build on this for the future. Conflict is a fact of life, so developing skilful ways of handling it will serve you well.

Conflict can be positive and healthy. The idea is not to avoid it but to recognise when it is potentially dysfunctional and to have the ability to adapt your own behaviour when necessary or to intervene skilfully to help others through the conflict to resolution.

CHAPTER 11

CREATING A SENSE OF PURPOSE AND MEANING

'Talent without unity of purpose is a hopelessly devalued currency.'
—Sir Alex Ferguson, Former Manager, Manchester United Football Club
(*The Independent*, 30 April 2011)

'Work is about a daily search for meaning as well as daily bread; for recognition as well as cash; for astonishment rather than torpor; in short for a sort of life, rather than a Monday-to-Friday sort of dying.'
—Studs Terkel, *Working,* 1970

INTRODUCTION

More and more research shows us that a sense of purpose and meaning is critical to effective teamwork and to a strong sense of belonging and involvement to the team or organisation. A recent McKinsey survey reported that nearly 90 per cent of those surveyed wanted purpose in their lives (Gast *et al.*, 2020). And 70 per cent said that their sense of purpose is largely defined by work. Interestingly, over 80 per cent of executives and upper management said they are living their values at work, while only 15 per cent of frontline managers and employees felt they were living their values at work. This represents both a danger and an opportunity. The danger is that people in your team who get less purpose from their work report less pride, satisfaction, commitment, engagement, connection and excitement at work. Clearly that is not ideal for effective performance. The opportunity is that if you can engage your people in reflecting on what gives them meaning at work and find opportunities for them to do meaningful work, then they will be more likely to show more pride, gain more satisfaction and be more engaged in their work.

Purpose is also good for business. For example, in a study carried out by Ernst and Young, two thirds of executives surveyed were profoundly rethinking their purpose as a result of disruption, and most of those (over 59 per cent) are moving toward a human-centred, socially engaged conception of purpose that seeks to create value for a broad set of stakeholders. Nearly 60 per cent of business leaders see purpose as being very important to their own personal job satisfaction (Ernst &Young, 2019).

WHAT IS PURPOSE?

The dictionary definition of purpose is *the reason anything is done or created and that which is relevant*. Relevance is the key word here. More and more team members are asking questions like:

- Is my work meaningful?
- Is it relevant?
- What is the purpose of my work?

WHY PURPOSE IS IMPORTANT

The need for purpose in our lives is nothing new. In his excellent book, *Flow, The Psychology of Optimal Experience,* Mihaly Csikszentmihalyi says, '*One cannot lead a life that is truly excellent without feeling that one belongs to something greater and more permanent than oneself'* (Csikszentmihalyi, 2008). A personal purpose statement is specific, clear and aligned to your values. It may only be a couple of sentences, but it defines who you are and your aspirations. It reflects what you are passionate about and helps guide you through life.

Steve Jobs' personal purpose wasn't to build the biggest computer company in the world. It was *'to make a contribution to the world by making tools for the mind that advance humankind'.* Clinical psychologist and author Jordan Peterson says that to have meaning in your life is better than to have what you want, because you may neither know what you want nor what you truly need (Peterson, 2018).

The American economist and Nobel prize winner Milton Friedmann famously stated that the sole responsibility of business was to make profits. On his death *The Economist* described him as the most influential economist of the second half of the twentieth century . . . possibly of all of it. Friedman has indeed been hugely influential – to the extent that for many years it was the norm for business to repudiate any other purpose apart from making profit. In Friedman's own words:

> *There is one and only one social responsibility of business – to use its resources and engage in activities designed to increase its profits so long as it stays within the rules of the game, which is to say, engages in open and free competition without deception or fraud.* (See www. wikipedia.org/wiki/friedman_doctrine)

Nowadays that thinking has changed radically, and it has become the norm for businesses to talk about the concept *of 'profit plus'.* This means that while they need to create profit to survive, it is not the sole reason for their existence. In fact, the UK's corporate governance code recognises the act of a purpose beyond profit; one of the rules in the code states that profit is not the purpose of a company but that profit is one outcome of identifying and pursuing a purpose that benefits society.

To illustrate this, in the UK, the Purposeful Company has gathered together 14 CEOs of major companies including Capita, Nat West, PWC and Unilever in order to demonstrate that having a purpose beyond the profit motive brings a variety of benefits including strategic clarity, operational discipline and more meaningful work for employees.

PURPOSE-LED ORGANISATIONS TEND TO BE MORE SUCCESSFUL

Babson professor and Whole Foods advisor, Raj Sisodia, studied 28 companies from 1996 to 2013 and concluded that purpose-driven enterprises grew by 1681 per cent compared to the Standard and & Poors 500 (this is the US stock market index which tracks 500 large companies listed on Stock Exchanges) average of 118 per cent (Sisodia, 2014).

The Global Leadership Forecast 2018 by DDI World (a global leadership consulting firm) finds that purposeful companies outperform the market by more than 40 per cent financially (Neal *et al.*, 2021).

And, going forward it will be important if you want to attract and retain the best talent to have a clear and meaningful sense of Purpose – not just a focus on profits alone. For example, more than 80 per cent of Gen Z in the US consider a company's purpose when deciding where to work (Cone, 2019) and four out of five US college graduates say it is very important or extremely important to derive a sense of purpose from their work. Interestingly, less than half of college graduates succeed in finding purposeful work. But those graduates are, however, almost ten times more likely to have high overall well-being (Gallup & Bates College, 2019).

Former Saracens Women's Rugby Football Club, England international and World Cup winner, Maggie Alphonsi, MBE, tells us that in a sports team – and in business – it's important to have shared vision and a common goal:

> *I think there has to be something that we all buy into and that allows you to move in a direction. If I think about the work that I do with Vitality – a health insurance company – we talk a lot about shared purpose and the importance of buying into that one goal. I think that's the same with a sports team, knowing that we all buy into one thing that allows us to have momentum – so yes we need a common purpose!* (Private communication with authors, 2022)

It's therefore pretty clear that working on meaning and purpose is going to be an important part of your work with the team.

THREE LEVELS OF PURPOSE

There are three levels at which you need to look for purpose, and these can have an impact on the successful engagement of your team.

- The first level is that of the individual team member.
- The second is at the team level.
- The third is at the organisational level.

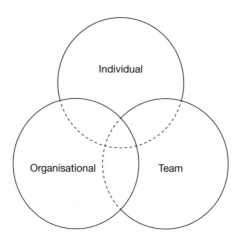

In an ideal world these three levels of purpose would overlap in order to ensure optimum performance from individuals, teams and the organisation overall. Let's look at each level.

INDIVIDUAL LEVEL

Let us share an example of what an individual mission or purpose statement can look like. Regan Gallo – Vice President of Architectural Solutions in the St Gobain group in the US – has developed a personal mission statement that summarises her purpose at work. It is '*To strive to create enabling conditions to help people do positive work and lead rewarding lives'.* (Personal communication with authors, 2021)

This reminds Regan why she goes to work, helps her focus on what her purpose is and communicates a clear message to her team members that she cares both about their work and also their lives.

The first step in developing purpose at the individual level is to ask your individual team members to reflect on what gives them meaning and purpose in their life, and how they can link that to their specific role. One way of doing this is to simply ask them what they do well. Ask them to list at least 20 things they do well at work – it's even better if you actually sit with them and keep asking the question. Or have your team members do it in pairs with each other. Then ask them to go through the list and write down:

- how they apply this in their job
- how it contributes to a sense of purpose.

If they can't make the link, between what they do well and how they apply it in their job, then simply ask them how they *could* apply it to their job.

The next step is for the team leader to find and create opportunities for team members to work on projects that are meaningful to that specific team member. Clearly that can't be done without the team leader knowing what is meaningful to each team member.

Linking values and purpose is another way of helping people to reflect on their purpose by looking at what they value. Once we have a clear sense of our values then it's much easier to reflect on and identify meaning and purpose. At this point you might like to reflect about your own values.

Perhaps list your top ten values from the list below, which is from The Barrett Values Centre (Barrett, 2017). This might help you to identify your own individual and possibly your team's values. The list is not exhaustive so feel free to add your own. Circle or highlight those values that you feel are most important to you. To help select your values you might ask yourself questions like:

- What must be present to make me feel fulfilled and happy?

- What values must I honour and never compromise on?

List of values (source: Barrett Values Centre)

Ambitious	Original	Democracy	Self-Respect	Goodwill
Autonomous	Perfection	Determined	Single-minded	Honour
Capable	Privacy	Expert	Tolerance	Innovative
Commitment	Radical	Family	Truth	Justice
Co-operation	Security	Fun	Wisdom	Love
Dedicated	Sincere	Honesty	Authentic	Open
Dependable	Teamwork	Independent	Brave	Peace
Empathetic	Trust	Integrity	Change	Power
Faithful	Variety	Leadership	Competence	Punctuality
Freedom	Adventurous	Money	Curiosity	Respect
Harmony	Benevolent	Patriotic	Decisiveness	Self-sufficient
Imaginative	Challenging	Pleasure	Egalitarian	Success
Inspiring	Community	Prosperity	Fair	Tranquil
Knowledge	Creativity	Reliability	Frank	Unique
Loyalty				

Once you have identified up to 10 values you believe to be most important to you, you can do the following steps:

- Rank them in order of importance with 1 being the most important.

- Describe what each value means to you and why it is important.

- Think about times when you have lived by and demonstrated your values and the outcomes and implications of doing so.

- Then think about when you have had to compromise on your values and the implications of this.

- Thinking about your values and the insights gained from this exercise, ask yourself how your current role lives up to this and how your team meets your needs.

- Finally consider doing the above as a team reflection.

The Barratt Values Centre has a really interesting questionnaire which you can find online, and which will help you identify your key values (https://valuescentre.com).

Another approach to thinking about values was developed by Professor Shalom Schwarz whose research identified 10 universal values.

- Benevolence – which is linked to helpfulness

- Achievement – this is about how you value success and ambition

- Self-direction – how creative you can be and how much freedom you want

- Hedonism – how much you want pleasure

- Universalism – this is about how much you value social justice and equality

- Security – this is about wanting social order

- Conformity – how much you value obedience

- Stimulation – how much you want and value an exciting life

- Tradition – how much you value and respect humility and devoutness

- Power – this is about how you value having authority and wealth.

We all value these things differently – so it's worthwhile thinking about which you value most and asking your team members to rank them in order of most important to least important.

As an example, in a small study we did in an international French company with 90 managers the top three values were:

- benevolence
- achievement
- self-direction.

The discussion was then based on how each *individual* interpreted these values specifically, and how they could use these values in their leadership. Each of the managers then undertook to do the same exercise with their teams. Clearly each team would have different rankings and therefore different sets of priorities when it came to values. But understanding each team's preferences allows you to have a meaningful conversation with each individual about values and purpose.

TEAM PURPOSE AND VALUES

Having identified each individual's values it is then useful for each team to sit down and reflect on their *team* purpose, and to create a purpose statement that is relevant at the team level. At this level, the purpose statement needs to have five key characteristics.

It needs to be:

1. Clear
2. Compelling
3. Challenging
4. Consequential

AND

5. It needs to be Agreed by the team.

Clear

Many purpose statements are worthy but vague. In a Kantar survey, three quarters of marketing heads were of the belief that their own organisation had a defined sense of purpose, but only one in ten could produce a corporate purpose statement and plan to back-up these beliefs (Kantar, 2018). Since the idea of the purpose statement is to give a clear intent and direction to the team's performance, vagueness isn't helpful. On the other hand, if the purpose is too defined and too narrow it then has no flexibility.

Compelling

The purpose must be something that is compelling for the team, that drives them forward and has real meaning for the team members. The purpose statement must take account of and build on each team member's individual purpose and meaning – which is where the values ranking is a useful exercise.

A purpose statement that mentions only numbers and figures is unlikely to be viewed as compelling, and therefore is unlikely to be effective.

Challenging

We know that motivation is likely to be higher if a task is neither too easy nor too difficult. Too easy and there just isn't enough satisfaction. If the task is too hard and we feel we have no chance of achieving it, then our motivation is reduced. Creating a team purpose that is challenging enough is what you need to aim for. In our interview with former England Cricket Captain, Sir Andrew Strauss, he explained:

> That idea of having a really bold ambitious goal we are all trying to achieve together, I think that has a benefit of everyone committing to something that's bigger than their own interests and gives them a reason to put in the work and the sacrifices that are needed to achieve that goal. So, a starting point is to find something that we are trying to do as a group of people that is ground-breaking and has never been done before. It is bold, ambitious and really excites people emotionally. I think to take them away from their own narrow concerns, insecurities and focus on something that is broader and bigger that at the end of their career they can go, you know what if we achieve this it will be something special. People talk about the 'Big Hairy Audacious Goal'. A really bold, ambitious goal is a fundamental starting point if you want a team to operate successfully. (Personal interview with authors, 2021)

Consequential

It's important for the team purpose to have positive consequences – not just for the team or organisation, but in a wider sense. It is unlikely that a purpose statement of increasing sales by 10 per cent year on year is consequential enough. And the purpose must have consequences in the sense that NOT adhering to the organisation's purpose must have some kind of implications for managers and employees. The purpose must be embedded in the organisation and team's culture, behaviours and decision making. Otherwise, there is a danger that the purpose becomes a meaning-less slogan like in so many organisations.

Agreed

None of the above will matter if the team doesn't agree on their purpose, so it is critical to ensure that everyone is on board. The process is fairly straightforward – you get the team together and you ask what the team does that contributes towards a sense of meaning and purpose in the team members' lives. (If each individual team member has completed the values ranking exercise this will be helpful.) This usually leads to an excellent conversation about what the team does that is meaningful and purposeful. The benefits of doing this collectively are that team members can build on each other's thoughts and ideas. If you feel that the responses are not particularly positive, and that there doesn't seem to be a lot that is contributing towards a strong sense of Purpose, then you can ask what *could* and *should* the team do – as a team – that would contribute towards a sense of purpose and meaning.

ORGANISATIONAL LEVEL

Both large and small companies are developing their sense of organisational purpose. We know that it's probably an easier process to do in a small company. An example of organisational purpose in a small company is Easy Jose Coffee in Shepton Mallet in England. They import 'shade' coffee grown by indigenous communities in the Amazon. 'Shade' coffee is grown beneath the forest canopy, in the shade, rather than in a clearing. Generally speaking, traditional coffee farms necessitate the clearance and destruction of the forest in order to plant coffee trees, while shade coffee doesn't. So Easy Jose's purpose is to '*help protect the rainforest, the indigenous Mayni community and provide excellent coffee*'. Their mission is to create sustainable personal relationships with indigenous producers who must show tangible results of forestry protection and uphold organic growing principles. Their investment provides the funds to benefit the local communities and helps protect their way of life (See their website at https://www.easyjosecoffee.co.uk/).

But even huge organisations are getting involved with Purpose and sometimes these are not organisations you would typically associate with any purpose other than making as much money as possible! One of these organisations is American investment bank J.P. Morgan. Their CEO and Chairman, Jamie Dimer, is quoted (from the *Guardian*, 8 April 2021) as saying, *'We are fully engaged in trying to solve some of the world's biggest issues – climate change, poverty, economic development and racial inequality'.* The reason he gives is that companies like J.P. Morgan, *'have an extraordinary capability to help not just with funding, but with developing strong public policy that can have a greater impact on public policy'.* J.P. Morgan has a somewhat chequered history, so it is telling that even a major investment banker is getting involved with solving key issues and not just focusing on profit. That means that your organisation, whether it is large or small, needs to be thinking about Purpose.

An organisational purpose statement is a sentence or two that describes a company's focus to its internal and external stakeholders. A purpose statement describes the overarching reason that the company exists and how it should conduct itself. It is developed by the Board, the Executive team with feedback from employees and wider stakeholder groups. Examples of short, focused and easy-to-understand purpose statements are the ones developed by the NASA Space Centre in the 1960s when the common purpose was *'to put a man on the moon', (sic)* and more recently Tesla's mission which focuses on increasing the pace of the world's shift to sustainable energy.

The organisational level is more complex in that you as an individual or team member have less input and control over the organisation's purpose. However, in order for team members to be fully engaged they do have to buy in, at least to some extent, to the organisation's purpose. The challenge here is for team leaders to help their team understand the wider purpose and to make explicit links between individual team members, purpose and the wider organisation purpose. You may also find that you need to influence upwards to help the organisation be more explicit about its purpose. Nigel has always believed that team purpose is critical and will define a team and highlight their difference to other teams. In sporting teams everyone wants to win the league, but creating a point of difference separates the team from the other teams in the league and provides something the whole team can buy into and draw collective strength from when times get tough.

When Nigel was Chief Executive of USA Rugby, the staff worked with the Chairman, Saatchi and Saatchi CEO Kevin Roberts, to develop a purpose for USA Rugby.

We spent a couple of days with staff and the board discussing the sport we loved and the impact it made on our lives. We discussed the joy of picking up a rugby ball for the first time and running with it, just as William Webb-Ellis must have done in 1832 when he created the sport. It was that special feeling that we wanted others to experience, we wanted kids to pick up the ball and run with it, we wanted to 'Inspire Americans to Fall In Love With Rugby' which led us to develop the award winning Rookie Rugby programme introducing thousands of young boys and girls to the game.

What is interesting is that USA rugby involved different levels of the organisation and their purpose leads directly to a specific set of actions – like the Rookie Rugby programme – the programme designed to introduce rugby to kids who had never before played the game.

REFLECTION

Finally, you may like to think about purpose in your working life – your organisation's, your team's and your own. Use the chart below to record purpose in each of the three specific areas. Consider the fit between the three areas. Are they in harmony? If not, what can you do about it? You can use this as a personal reflection or as a team exercise. It's a really effective conversation to have in your team and you should be able to make some explicit links between team members' individual values, the team values and the organisation's values and purpose.

Organisation	Team	Personal

CHAPTER 12

THE IMPORTANCE OF FEEDBACK AND ACCOUNTABILITY

'We all need people who will give us feedback. That's how we improve.'

Bill Gates

'I think it's very important to have a feedback loop, where you are constantly thinking about what you've done and how you could be doing it better.'

Elon Musk

INTRODUCTION

In this chapter we will explore the importance of feedback and accountability for effective performance. We will discuss how to create a culture of feedback, the elements of good-quality feedback and the link between feedback, performance and accountability and we will suggest effective processes you can apply in your work.

Nigel believes that in sport it is clear that feedback is what differentiates average performers from high-performance or elite performers. High-performance sportsmen and women always have a strong culture of feedback, where coaches, managers and athletes are all bought into the feedback process as a key element in building success. However, in our collective experience this is not always the case in organisational life.

In a high-performance sports team, performance is constantly analysed. And as a member of that team, you are constantly receiving feedback, not just from your boss as is typical in business, but from everyone. You get feedback from your friends, family, from the fans, and from the media, as well as from your captain, coach and colleagues! You even get feedback from people who didn't see the game! The kind of feedback where when you go into a shop to get your paper the shop owner will tell you 'I heard you had a shocker last night!' Or more positively, 'I heard you had a great match last night'.

An openness to feedback and being willing and able to receive feedback is a necessity for a member of any successful sports team. Sportsmen and women who are unwilling to receive feedback are highly unlikely to make it to elite performance level. According to former British Olympic athlete Kriss Akabussi, a feedback culture is an essential part of the high-performance athlete's environment (Private communication with authors, 2021). Kriss is an Olympic bronze and silver medallist and also has a world championship gold medal – so he knows a thing or two about high performance. He believes that without effective feedback an athlete cannot fully realise their potential and that it's exactly the same in a business or organisational environment.

In business and in organisational teams, feedback is much rarer, and it tends not to be part of the culture, as people are not quite so comfortable giving or receiving feedback. Analysis of performance and feedback is critical for high performance, so it's essential that team members and team leaders become more comfortable and skilful at giving and receiving feedback. We have developed a model which illustrates the link between feedback accountability and performance:

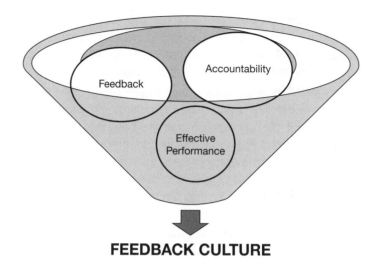

FEEDBACK CULTURE

FEEDBACK

Research has shown that people at work want to give and receive feedback in order to understand and contribute to better overall performance. So, let's look in more depth at how to give and receive feedback. Three things are needed in terms of feedback in order to maximise performance:

1. A culture where feedback is integral.
2. People who can and will give feedback in a skilful way.
3. People who accept and seek feedback.

CREATING A CULTURE OF FEEDBACK

This will contribute to the overall morale, productivity and personal performance in any organisation. Leaders at all levels will play a major role in creating a feedback culture. In essence a culture of feedback means that all employees feel that they can share feedback with another person in their workplace regardless of that person's position or role. While this is a challenge, there are a range of features that need to exist or if they don't, they need to be introduced to begin the process of developing a feedback culture. These include:

- Leaders must **model** good feedback behaviour by asking people for feedback about their own performance. One useful way of doing this is to ask people, when you are chatting to them about a project they are working on, what you could do to help them progress things? In this way you are encouraging someone to talk about your behaviour and to suggest better ways of working together.

- Leaders should be **generous** in their praise and positive feedback to others. Not simply saying things like *'thank you great job'* or *'well done'* but actually explaining what's been done well, why and how it affected you and the team. So, something like *'you did a great job winning that business, they are a difficult client to please and you seem to have recognised their needs and put things in place to make sure they get what they need from the whole team.'*

- Leaders should **talk** to their colleagues and team members about feedback and how it can contribute to their environment. Engage in a conversation with all those involved to be clear about everyone's views about feedback and how it might work in your organisation. Agree some ground rules with your team about what will work for you and what won't.

- **Create processes** for giving and receiving feedback in your organisation. By building feedback into the day-to-day work you are far more likely to be successful in creating a transparent culture of feedback. Some of the processes might be:

  - regular reviews during and at the end of meetings/projects to ensure all is going well and to learn from experience
  - schedule feedback discussions on a regular basis with all team members
  - make sure feedback is two way – it is not only the leaders' job to give feedback but to actively ask for it also.

Creating a culture of feedback will take time and effort but in the long run it will lead to a more collaborative culture where high performance is the norm. One good example of gold-standard feedback was shared with us by the English Rugby Football Union's Professional Referees, under the leadership of Tony Spreadbury, the head of professional referees at the English Rugby Football Union headquartered at Twickenham Stadium in London.

EXAMPLE

Tony and his team of mentors who are all former referees have developed a strong and robust feedback culture. The way it works is: Once the professional referees have finished their game, they travel to the RFU headquarters at Twickenham and stay there for two days to review and critique their performance. Each referee meets one on one with their mentor and reviews their whole match on video. The referee has to point out both what they did well and where they could have done better. Their mentor will intervene and also point out areas of effectiveness and improvement – so it is a two-way process. If the referee doesn't spot an area for improvement and the mentor does, then they will step in and point it out. The process is very detailed as both the referee and his mentor will have taken extensive notes before the meeting.

Once this part of the process is finished then the referees' panel (the mentors plus Tony) will have a private discussion in order to highlight specific actions and/or learning that can be of use to the referees. After this the referees will come into the meeting. You now have the referees and mentors in a session which is facilitated by Tony. Each referee has to stand up individually and comment on their game, highlighting anything they think they did well, and their mistakes and what they could improve. They also demonstrate this to their peers by showing them the video clips of the situation. Any so-called red flags (issues which are deemed to be of interest to and relevant to the whole group) are taken into this meeting, shared and then discussed by the whole team. The referee, having had feedback from the players, the fans and the media, and sometimes even the rugby clubs too, during and after the game, has to go through this detailed and specific process, getting feedback from both their mentor, their peers and Tony. The feedback is not always fun, sometimes the referee has made a fairly major mistake and then has to take the feedback from their colleagues in the session. At the end Tony will summarise the session and make recommendations to the referees.

This comprehensive and open review leads to a culture of continuous improvement and high performance which is essential given the high stakes and constant scrutiny.

This type of video feedback is increasingly used by elite sports people to help them to understand and improve their performance. Now videoing meetings at work and so on might be a step too far for most workplaces, but the essence of review remains one of the key elements of building a successful feedback culture as well as developing skill in both giving and receiving feedback.

REFLECTION

Think about the above example and identify any elements of the process that you could introduce and apply in your own team.

GIVING FEEDBACK

This is a skill that many people find quite stressful. Working in an environment where feedback is part of the culture will certainly help lessen the stress. However, it still requires skills; these can be learned and developed. Following a few simple rules is a good starting point for this development and in this area, practise certainly makes it easier.

- Make sure feedback is given in a **timely** manner. By this we mean it should be done on a regular basis or shortly after the event you wish to praise or offer constructive feedback about. Allow enough time for a discussion to take place; it's also important for feedback conversations to be two-way. Allocate enough time to explore and plan how to incorporate the feedback into future performance whether it is building on success or developing a less developed area.

- Be **specific** by focussing on the exact event or issue you wish to provide feedback about. The feedback giver must avoid being vague. For instance: if you wish to praise someone for their contribution to a meeting do it speedily after the meeting and talk about what in particular you valued about their contributions. If on the other hand you wish to provide constructive feedback, be clear about what they need to improve and then ask them how they think they could do better and agree a pathway for improvement.

- **Regular** feedback is one of the main contributors towards people being open to feedback and to creating a feedback culture. Build feedback into day-to-day work, for instance, after team meetings. You could begin to institute processes whereby after any team meeting each participant is encouraged to:

○ Say one thing that went well in the meeting and one thing that could be improved.

○ Turn to the person on their left and offer them one piece of positive feedback about their contribution to the meeting. Once people get used to this process – say after a couple of times – then you can build in a second round where team members give everyone a piece of development feedback.

Leaders should be encouraged to instigate regular meetings (at least four times a year) with their direct reports where they offer an opportunity for discussion about what's going well/not so well for them.

■ Feedback should be **balanced** with a focus on both the positive and developmental. Feedback should also be given when you know the feedback recipient is willing to listen and act upon it. This will require a degree of empathy and knowledge about the person. Of course, if a culture of feedback exists in the workplace then this will make both giving and receiving feedback easier.

■ **Prepare** for the conversations, what you wish to say and how you wish to say it and remember you must focus on behavioural change not a person's personality. For instance: **Do Not** say something like – '*you are so arrogant you always think you are right*'. It is much better to say something like '*When you imply that your way is best in meetings, it stops others offering their ideas. How could you adapt to accommodate other colleagues' perspectives?*'

Think about where you will have the feedback session: for instance, if the feedback is developmental or constructive then make sure it is done in private. It is also worth considering the person involved as some people are happy to receive positive feedback in an open forum, while others prefer even positive feedback in private. Check with your individual team colleagues how they prefer to receive feedback.

Fatima, a senior manager in a Middle Eastern bank, told us that in her opinion, feedback is the most important criterion for a leader in her environment (Private communication with authors, 2020). But she notices that managers often find it really difficult to give feedback. The problem has been that too often giving feedback is synonymous with giving negative feedback.

When your boss tells you that they want to give you some feedback, how do you feel? It's rare that team members look forward to receiving feedback. And feedback is all too often delivered in a very unskilled manner. The feedback is either too vague and general (for example, 'people are saying' or is focused on the negatives without any consideration of strengths or accomplishments.

Consider this quote from Adrian Moorhouse, former Olympic swimmer and currently Managing Partner of EY/Lane 4, a management development and training consultancy:

> If relationships are too cosy within the organisation it might lead to a lack of confronting and challenging. You have to be able to say what you think in a respectful way of course. . . So, it is necessary to give feedback, and people must become skilled in how to give effective feedback. I worry that tough unskilful feedback might destroy relationships, so I feel that the way feedback is delivered is critical. You might have some tough feedback to give but if it is given in a skilled, effective way it should not only improve performance but also improve the relationship. (Private communication with authors, 2019)

Before we move onto receiving feedback, one final thought about giving feedback is that training your people in both processes for giving and receiving will be time usefully spent and will add to the commitment to feedback and the overall culture in the organisation.

When we run a development session about feedback, we use the mnemonic BOOST to help people remember the key components of good feedback.

B – BALANCED

O – OWNED

O – OBSERVED

S – SPECIFIC

T – TIMELY

RECEIVING FEEDBACK

One of the main problems here is that many people do not want feedback and they become defensive when given feedback.

One international sportswoman told us, 'Nobody likes feedback ! Well … good feedback – we all love that, but we don't like bad feedback!'

This of course can be a normal reaction when the feedback is poorly delivered and if there is not an accepted culture of feedback within the organisation. A typical reaction here is to go into defensive routines of the 'it wasn't me it was him' type, or come up with many excuses as to why things are as they are and even to go into complete denial. If a person is not willing to receive, accept and work on feedback, then the problem is probably due to a lack of clarity about the culture and values of the organisation or team and having had experience of poorly delivered feedback at some point.

Some of the key elements you will need to receive and understand feedback given to you by others include:

- **Ask others for feedback** – this certainly indicates to others that you want to hear from them about your performance or contribution. It could be because you are unsure about a particular skill or ability or you may simply wish to understand how others perceive you. We find that one of the best ways of doing this so that you get feedback of value and meaning is to be specific. For instance, if you have a concern about how your body language is perceived, ask someone you trust to observe you in a meeting and provide you with feedback on how you use your body language and how it is perceived during the meeting. Being specific makes it easier for the feedback giver and means you are more likely to get specific comments in return rather than a generalised comment such as '*it's ok*'.

- Demonstrating a willingness to **actively listen** by turning off your immediate and instinctive emotional response and asking yourself questions like '*what is this person trying to tell me?*' or '*why is this important to me?*'. By doing this you will be more objective and in control. You may also show that you are listening by summarising back to the feedback giver what you have heard and what you understand by it.

- **Probing for understanding**, by asking open questions, especially if you are not clear about the main point of the feedback. Typically, at this stage you will be checking out what they mean and what might work better in the future.

- **Sharing how you plan to move ahead**. Once you fully understand the feedback and have thought through what you will do about it, show the feedback giver that you are going to take some or all of their feedback on board and try out some new ways of working – stating specifically what these might be.

- **Show appreciation** to the feedback giver by thanking them. This will demonstrate that you valued their thoughts and will encourage them to give you feedback again in the future.

One way of helping people become more comfortable accepting feedback is to introduce a process where colleagues are encouraged to share feedback after a team meeting. When we run training sessions about developing feedback skills, we often deploy the technique of focused feedback to ensure people take away some learning from any group discussions they have. This works by asking them to discuss, for example 'What contributes to good-quality feedback?'. We then ask them to review their discussion by giving each other feedback on:

- What went well?
- What should they stop doing?
- What can they do differently next time they meet?

By encouraging this sort of structured process, you are helping people to develop the skills of giving and receiving feedback as well as building a culture of feedback.

ACCOUNTABILITY

Mutual accountability is one of the hallmarks of a high-performing team. Team members recognise that taking joint responsibility for their actions, behaviours and achievements leads to mutual trust, a joint commitment to goals and a happy ship.

Building an environment where team members feel mutually accountable is not always easy. Colleagues can lean on others, become complacent and when it all goes wrong, try to shift the blame elsewhere. That clearly wouldn't be a tenable situation in many organisations, for instance in the military, where in high-stakes circumstances, accountability is crucial. Former British Army Officer and Sandhurst instructor Dominic Mahoney emphasises the important role that reviewing and reflecting has to play in building accountability in a military team. He points out that after a training exercise, or a real engagement with the enemy, the team will **always** review what happened (Private communication with authors, 2018). The questions will be based on the following:

- What did we set out to do?
- What happened?
- What did we learn?
- What will we do better next time?

It's a practice that is built into all military training – and one that Dominic believes could be usefully replicated by business teams. He believes that teamwork in the corporate world is often sloppy, partly because teams are *'wrapped up in cotton'* and unlike in the military, mistakes don't usually have life threatening consequences. So, what can the business and organisational world learn from the military about creating empowered teams where people feel both individually and jointly responsible for what they do and how they behave?

- **Make accountability integral.** If you want people to take responsibility, accountability has to be an integral part of an organisation's culture and DNA. It needs to become an essential part of 'the way we do things around here'. This is particularly important in the intimate environment of smaller organisations, where a lack of trust or motivation is felt company-wide and can have a long-lasting impact. Team leaders have to take responsibility for creating a culture where accountability is a natural process for both individuals and the team as a whole, just as it is in the British Army.

- **Encourage discussion and involvement.** If you want to inspire commitment, it is important to hear what the team itself has to say. Be sure to allow an opportunity for discussion about targets and goals. Allow team members to contribute their ideas and thoughts, so that they feel truly empowered and feel they have the authority to act in relation to their responsibilities.

- **Contextualise.** Make sure people are fully aware of the organisation's purpose and vision, so that they can understand the role of their team and see how they personally fit in. This should be a constant dialogue, where people are kept up to date and encouraged to discuss and share ideas and opinions.

- **Be clear about expectations.** Be clear about your expectations of both the individuals in the team and the team as a whole. This includes being clear about consequences for both achievements and, most importantly, non-achievement. It is at this stage that there is a lot of scope for misunderstanding, so be explicit when stating your expectations.

- **Set targets and goals.** Clarify individual goals, targets and objectives. Ensure everyone fully understands their role and responsibilities and is aware that they will be held personally accountable for achieving their own contribution as well as the overall team goal.

- **Review.** Frequent reviews of both the process and progress against targets are vital for creating a culture of feedback and accountability and building trust and mutual respect. One idea implemented by the military is to introduce 'bite-sized' reviews at the end of each team meeting, to go quickly over lessons learned and to ensure better performance next time.

FEEDBACK AND ACCOUNTABILITY CULTURE

Investing time and energy in developing and creating a culture of feedback and accountability will lead to greater empowerment in your organisation and teams. Training people in the necessary skills and capabilities, and being adaptable to change and open to feedback will all lead to a feedback and accountability culture which will in turn lead to effective high levels of performance from both individuals and teams and will contribute to the overall culture of the organisation.

From the world of high-performance sport, rugby player Maggie Alphonsi emphasises the importance of having a culture of feedback and accountability.

At the national level – for the England team – we had regular feedback and I felt there was a lot of accountability. Before 2010, at the previous World Cup if things didn't go well, we were more likely as a team to pass the buck and say things like, 'It's your fault!'.

We might not necessarily point at individual team mates, but as players we might say to the coaches, 'You didn't do this!' And they would say, 'Well as players you probably weren't doing that!'.

It felt like it was an us versus them clash type of environment. But in 2014 it felt like that we took accountability. You held yourself accountable if you weren't doing things, or pulling your weight in terms of training and skill development. You wanted to take ownership and you felt it was very well managed and there was a balance.

The key thing here was that the team had worked together with the coaches and management on creating that culture of feedback and accountability, and it will be the same for you and your team. You need to have these open and honest conversations and create a culture where everyone can take responsibility and hold themselves accountable.

CHAPTER 13

COACHING THE INDIVIDUAL AND TEAMS

'A good coach can change a game. A great coach can change a life.'
John Wooden, US Basketball Coach and Player

INTRODUCTION

Whether you are a leader, a manager or a team member, coaching is fast becoming one of the key skills that drive high-performing teams. Research tells us that coaching by an executive's manager is the strongest factor in preparing them to move into leadership positions. The Chartered Institute of Personnel and Development in the UK, a leading research body, says that coaching by line managers is one of the most effective learning and talent development practices. Interestingly, their survey also suggests that it is one of the key leadership skills that organisations lack! (Baron, 2013). Research at Ashridge Executive Education also identifies coaching to be heavily favoured as a management style by Generation Y (Schofield, 2011).

It's clear from research and practice that a team leader will benefit enormously by being able to coach effectively. The dilemma is that coaching the team presents complications that are not present when coaching individuals. Teams have different dynamics to individuals, and so we must be able to coach the team as a whole entity, but without forgetting to address the needs of the individual members of that team. In this chapter we will look at the general skills of coaching, then address some of the specifics around coaching a team.

It is also important to mention that coaching is not simply the preserve of the leader or manager. Any team member can take on a coaching role, in fact in any high-performing team where members bring different skills and capabilities to the team and its work, the team members will probably be skilled in coaching each other. So, this chapter is aimed at team leaders and members alike.

THE BASICS OF COACHING

Before thinking specifically about coaching the team, you need to be able to acquire the basic skills and processes of coaching. The model below illustrates a summary of the essential basic skills of coaching.

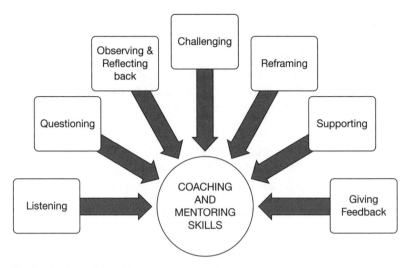

The basic skills of coaching
(Brent and Dent, 2015)

In the diagram above we have listed the basic skills of coaching, whether it be for the individual or the team. What follows is a brief summary of each of these skills:

LISTENING

This is one of the most difficult of all the skills, and one of the greatest opportunities. We all assume that we are good listeners, but this is not true: we sometimes treat a conversation like a game of ping pong – you speak, then I speak, and when you are speaking, I am thinking what to say next. That is not listening!

The great American psychologist Carl Rogers said that the tendency to react to any emotionally meaningful statement by forming an evaluation of it from our own perspective is the major barrier to interpersonal communication (Rogers, 2011, 2012). So, if you do not listen carefully and attentively to what a team member is saying, and listen also to what is *not* said, then not only do you risk missing out on an important contribution but also you will negatively impact your relationship with that team member. If you are not listening, they know it.

Here is an exercise you can try with your team when you are having a reflection or development session. Do this ideally in a group of four. It can also be adapted to be done in groups of three. In this case one person listens for both feelings and intentions/assumptions.

EXERCISE

Person A speaks for 2 minutes or so, uninterrupted, about a current problem or issue they are dealing with. The others all listen at the different levels we describe below, and then take turns to reflect back to the speaker what they heard – at each level.

Person B will listen for **THINKING**. We call this level 1 listening. What sort of words are chosen? What data have been used? What logic and analysis have been applied? What judgements and opinions have been made?

Person C will listen for **FEELINGS**. We call this level 2 listening. How are they feeling right now? How did they feel at the time? What was their non-verbal communication?

Person D will listen for **INTENTIONS AND ASSUMPTIONS**. We call this level 3 listening. What do they intend to do about it? What is the level of commitment to this action? What assumptions might they be making?

The listeners then share with the speaker, *Person A*, what they heard, and the speaker tells each listener how accurate they were. By hearing their conversation back at the three levels the speakers are able to reflect more deeply about their issues.

This exercise will illustrate several important aspects of the listening process. Attentive, effective listening is a sophisticated process involving more than simply hearing words. To be effective you need to listen at a logical or thinking level for the quality of the language used, the evidence given, and any judgements and opinions offered. You need to have the ability to pick up and understand the feelings the speaker displays whether it is through their words or non-verbal communication. Finally, did the speaker give any indication of their intentions or assumptions from either what they say or how they say it?

This is an exercise we often use with executives on our training courses to illustrate the complexity of the listening process. Many people tell us they find it instructive in helping them to understand how they can further develop their listening skills. Typically, people can identify the levels of listening they find most easy and the most challenging and therefore can practise the latter.

For effective coaching to take place you need to be able to listen at all three levels and to show the speaker that you are doing so by reflecting back to them in a summary to check you have understood their point.

QUESTIONING

Asking the right questions creates focus and clarity. An open and probing question will bring an interesting and insightful response, whereas the response to a closed question will be 'Yes' or 'No'! The purpose of the question is to encourage team members to open up and offer their opinions and suggestions and also to share their genuine views and feelings. The intent of the coach must be to fully understand their team members' perspectives. They should use a full range of questioning techniques to suit each coaching situation. For example, there are Open questions, Probing questions, Reflective questions, Funnel questions and Closed questions. They all have their uses depending on the situation.

OBSERVING AND REFLECTING BACK

It is important to notice what is going on with the team and individuals' body language and paralinguistics or vocal usage. Research tells us that a great deal of the meaning of any communication comes through non-verbal communication – body language and paralinguistics. So, it is important to listen beyond the words that are said and use your eyes as well as ears to notice what is really going on. Pay attention to the coherence between what is said and *how* it is said and be prepared to challenge any discrepancies. If you feel that someone's words are not congruent with their body language or facial expression then check it out, probe a bit further by reflecting back what you are seeing and what you are hearing. For instance, someone may say they agree with you, but their facial expression is indicating to you some doubt. Better to check this out before moving on to ensure you are gaining commitment to whatever they agree with.

REFRAMING

According to Amy C Edmondson, Professor of Leadership and Management at Harvard Business School (Edmondson, 2014), a frame is a set of assumptions or beliefs about a situation. As a team coach you need to know what your team's assumptions are about a particular situation; then you can either support or challenge that thinking appropriately. It's also critical for the team coach to be able to offer helpful re-frames of situations.

For example, in 2019, in a Six Nations rugby match against England at England's home ground Twickenham, Scotland were losing 31 points to 7 at half time. They appeared totally beaten and demoralised and it looked as if the second half could only bring more of the same. However, in the second half Scotland proceeded to score five tries and towards the end of the game were actually leading by 38 points to 31. Only a last-minute try allowed England to come back and achieve a draw. According to newspaper reports, Scotland's coach together with the team captain and senior players reframed the situation. Instead of focusing on what was going badly and blaming each other, they reframed the objective as winning the second half and achieving respect. By focusing on what was possible in the future and not on what they had done badly, they were able to find the necessary energy and confidence to salvage a match which everyone thought was lost.

Can you think about a situation in your own life where you have 'reframed' an event to make it more positive and therefore re-energised you?

CHALLENGING

It is essential in teams to be able to challenge one another's thinking, and it's also important for team members to be able to challenge the leaders' thinking. We live in a world where many of the problems any team has to face are so-called '*Wicked*' problems. These are problems that have no right or wrong answer – only better or worse options. The concept of so-called 'wicked' problems was created by two American professors back in the 1970s but it is entirely appropriate in today's VUCA (volatile, uncertain, complex and ambiguous) environment, where more and more of the issues we face have no single solution. Many UK businesses in the last few years have been posed the 'wicked' problem of planning for how best to deal with BREXIT, a situation that is new to all with no previous history to draw on. Another example of a wicked problem that many teams are working on is climate change and how best to plan ahead.

Historically it was thought that the team leader had all the answers, and the team would follow their direction, but more recently leadership has become more focused on collaboration. Today a collaborative leader is more likely to draw out all the options from the team, facilitate a conversation, ask questions to challenge the options and listen to the answers before they move on to set the direction based on the collective intelligence of the team. In these circumstances, it is highly unlikely that any team leader will have the best option for action without consulting the individual and collective intelligence of the team.

SUPPORTING

It is important for any coach to be able to offer support and encouragement to all team members. Creating the right environment for such interactions is important. Not every team member will be confident to speak up freely, and if you want to encourage freedom of thought and expression without fear of judgment which you should, of course, then you must be supportive of team members' participation, even if their ideas are not always brilliant. Creating opportunities for the team to express their views without fear of ridicule or recrimination is essential to build strong bonds between the team members themselves and with their leadership.

Being supportive in a team means listening to each other's points of view and ideas, summarising all the ideas and then agreeing which of these to action for moving forward to create a winning team.

One way of supporting your team might be to use smaller groups to discuss different ways of doing things. This provides the opportunity for those people who are reluctant to share in big groups of people to share their thoughts more openly in the smaller group and then for all views to be fed back into the bigger group.

GIVING FEEDBACK

This is a necessary element in coaching high-performing teams and all members of the team should be involved, both in giving and receiving feedback.

For truly effective teamwork it is important to develop a 'feedback culture'. Good quality feedback from teammates and the leader will contribute to each person's performance. So, what is good quality feedback? (Also see Chapter 12 on feedback and accountability.) Firstly, getting the balance right between appreciative and constructive feedback is a key element for success here. Research has shown that there should be a higher ratio of positive, appreciative feedback than negative or 'constructive' feedback. We have all experienced the so-called s**t sandwich, where the leader first gives positive feedback immediately followed by some negative feedback. This of course usually negates any positive energy the recipient has taken from the positive feedback. They then finish by giving another piece of positive feedback, in order not to leave the team member on a low note. But the team member is still dwelling on the negative feedback and doesn't really hear the final positive. There is absolutely no need to use this method of feedback, where you always link the positive with the negative. It's like saying, '*You're a really good team member BUT. . . .*'. People will only remember the BUT!

Good feedback practice involves getting into the habit of looking for the positives and sharing these with each other. So, when you see someone doing something well you should tell them – positive feedback. Then, when you see something you think isn't being done well, start by asking them, '*How do you think you did in that task?*'. Give the individual a chance to give themselves feedback before you jump in and criticise. This doesn't mean that skilled feedback givers simply focus on the positive rather it means you use a range of skills to help people understand what works and what doesn't.

COACHING MODELS AND PROCESSES

There are many different models and processes that teams can use in order to have a structured approach for coaching each other. Here we offer a summary of three models which we have found useful in coaching both individuals and teams. These are:

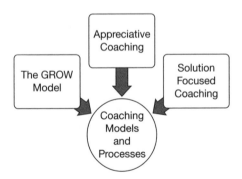

- The **GROW** model was developed by the late John Whitmore (2010) as a coaching framework to help people structure their coaching conversations.
- **Appreciative Coaching** is adapted from *Appreciative Inquiry* developed by David Cooperrider and Suresh Srivastva (Cooperrider et al., 2008).

■ **Solution Focused Coaching** is adapted from The Solution Focused approach developed by Steve de Shazer and Insoo Kim Berg as a therapeutic model (de Shazer et al., 2021).

THE GROW MODEL

This model can be used to coach both individual team members and also the team as a whole. The process focusses on four areas – **Goals, Realities, Options and Will (GROW)**. The idea is that the coach first of all explores each person's specific goals and objectives for the session, and then moves on to exploring what is going on in reality, what has been happening, what people have done and said, who is involved and so on. The coach then asks the coachee to develop a number of different options, before moving on to asking about the degree of will or commitment, and what energy the coachee has in order to take specific actions.

The GROW model helps you to take a more structured coaching approach rather than just giving advice or offering ideas to the coachee. In reality many managers start to coach without having fully explored the specific goals each team member or team has as a whole. They can then find themselves stuck without goals to focus on and there can then be no specific actions.

We have created a modified version of this structure and added an 'I' and a couple more Rs to the process. The **I** stands for **issue**. Clearly the coachee will need to explain their issue before the coach can ask for their goals. The first extra **R** reminds us to specifically ask about **relationships** as well as for facts and figures.

■ What are the feelings in the team?
■ What is the emotional reality?
■ Who else is involved and how are they feeling?

There is a real danger that managers will be tempted to skip the emotional realities involved! But it is the emotions, not logic, which lead to action. The other **R** we add is for **Resources**, by which we mean what are the strengths and resources that will help each coachee to move forward. When have they been successful in addressing similar issues for example? What are the resources and competences that will help them resolve the issue? You cannot focus simply on what the coachee or team cannot do!

Our version of the GROW model is illustrated below:

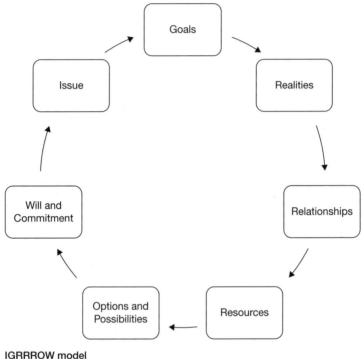

IGRRROW model
(adapted from Sir John Whitmore)

Following this process will help any coach to work through issues in a thorough and structured manner ensuring that all bases have been covered and will lead to greater levels of commitment for coaches to put their plan into action. It will help coaches to move away from the often-observed temptation to skip over the goals and go directly to reality questions. Typically, managers are very good at asking analytical questions concerning reality but are not so good at asking about the emotional and psychological realities. As for options, the trap that many managers fall into is to give *their* options and opinions rather than ask the coachee for theirs. Many people also forget to ask about will and commitment, assuming that it will just somehow happen! It is important to ask specific questions about the degree of will and commitment and to get specific actions and dates and to follow up on these.

APPRECIATIVE COACHING

This approach to coaching is based on a theory called Appreciative Inquiry (AI). Appreciative Inquiry was developed in the 1980s by David Cooperrider and Suresh Srivastva, two professors at the Weatherhead School of Management at Case Western Reserve University. Its basic premise is that it is a way to work with groups and individuals to focus on the positive and how this can be used to create a way forward for future effectiveness.

Appreciative Coaching basically looks at what is working well for team members and teams in general, so that they can imagine what might be possible for greater effectiveness and moving ahead. Teams can then co-create the desired future together. It builds on the positives rather than the negatives and is an excellent way of harnessing energy and looking at what the team might achieve going forward. More and more organisations are using the power of Appreciative Coaching.

We suggest the following process when using Appreciative Coaching.

- Start by enquiring about strengths and resources rather than probing into what is *not* working well in the team. You can also help team members to integrate any positive experiences and feedback they may already have. Too often the positives get ignored and team members can get into the bad habits of focusing exclusively on what's going wrong, the negatives and blaming others.

- Ask the team to imagine a better future or desired state. Where does the team *want* to get to? Get them to visualise their preferred future and then share it.

- Help the team to work through the specific actions and behaviours team members need to put in place in order to achieve their desired outcomes. Involve the team members here and get them to list specific behaviours, and make sure you record the list of behaviours so that you can come back and review against them.

- Ensure that review is part of the process, specifically how the team are progressing in their goals, objectives and behaviours.

SOLUTION FOCUSED COACHING

This approach takes the perspective of focussing on the way ahead and in particular on solutions not problems. The idea of solution focus was initially developed as a therapeutic model but has been adapted in recent years for coaching. It aims to help coachees find solutions, build on strengths and find ways forward.

Underlying this approach there are some basic assumptions and principles.

- **Change is happening all the time**, so the coach's job is to identify and amplify useful change. The coach therefore needs to inquire where useful change has already taken place within the team. If there is no evidence of useful change in the team then it's unlikely that the desired change will actually happen.

- **There is no one 'right' way of looking at things**: different views may fit the facts just as well. The coach's role here is to challenge assumptions and perceptions and explore different ways of thinking and perceiving. This helps to avoid 'groupthink' where certain people dominate the discussion and the others are afraid to speak up and challenge in the moment, even though they are pretty sure the idea is a bad or even catastrophic one.

- **Detailed understanding of the 'problem' is usually little help in arriving at the solution.** The coach does not have to spend huge amounts of time trying to understand the issues in great detail. Rather his or her job is to ask good open questions in order to help the team reflect on and become more aware of their issues. This can be helpful when experts and specialists dominate the team and just want to give their answer to the problem. It does however mean that the person doing the coaching has to let go of trying to find the answer and solving the problem themselves. The idea is that they step back from their subject expertise and allow the team members to reflect for themselves.

- **No 'problem' happens all the time.** There are always times when the problem is NOT happening, so a useful way forward lies in identifying what is going on when the problem does not occur. Again, the coach's role is to probe into when things are going well rather than when they are going badly. This can be unexpectedly difficult as the teams are often focused on the problem and find it difficult to turn their attention to what is positive. This approach is especially useful in working with change. Look for the areas where the 'problem' is not happening (or where the good things are happening) and see what's actually working. Then encourage the team to do more of this!

- **Small changes in the right direction can be amplified to great effect.** There seems to be a desire within organisations to effect big changes. But big changes are hard to achieve in reality. The Solution

Focused approach stresses the importance of recognising and encouraging when the team are taking small steps that are going in the right direction. So, it's much better to actually take a small step rather than make some over ambitious leap which is probably destined to fail. Unfortunately, we seem to be keen on big statements and audacious goals which don't actually work.

■ **It is useful to have the team imagine what a preferred future might look like.** This takes the form of the so-called 'Miracle' question where the coach asks the team (or individual team members) to imagine they have gone to bed and woken up the next day and a miracle has happened. Then the coach asks them to describe what is now happening. This is also quite a difficult technique, as often the coachee can resist the question and say that it is too difficult to answer or become defensive and say that a miracle can't possibly happen. But it's worth persisting and getting the coachee to use their imagination and visualise their preferred future. Once they have done this, it becomes easier for the team member to start describing the specific behaviours they will display in that future.

In the Solution Focused approach, it isn't necessary to delve into the roots of the problem or analyse the problem in detail. The focus, as its name suggests, is towards developing Solutions, and in particular the team's own solutions.

The Solution Focused Methodology. This is achieved through a variety of steps and processes which involve firstly finding the **Platform** – that is what are we here to do today? Then you can move to **Counters**, which means asking about the coachee's strengths and resources. What do they have that will help them overcome their issue? Then you would ask **Scaling** questions – in other words where are they on a scale of 1 to 10, with 10 being high? If for example the coachee says they are a 3 then you can ask where they would like to be. What would it be like if they were at 5? What would they be doing? What would they be saying? What would they be feeling?

Then finally you would move on to asking about what small steps the coachee could take in the right direction. This should be followed by positive affirmations to the coachee about the small steps before asking them to try out this different way of doing things before your next session.

COACHING THE TEAM

Much of what we have learned about coaching can be attributed to coaching in sport. Whether it be coaching a team – maybe football or rugby – or coaching individuals – tennis players or swimmers for example – we can learn much from sports coaching. So what are the transferable principles from team performance in sport to team performance in organisations?

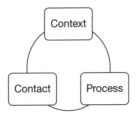

According to research by Dr Mark Lowther of Cardiff Metropolitan University's School of Sport, there are three key transferable principles of team coaching (Personal communication, 2020). These are Context, Processes and Contact.

As there might be less time for personal coaching in a team context, team coaching should be more about processes and less about individual feelings and emotions. There may be an assumption in the team that each individual already has a personal coach. The team coach would be looking at the individual's role in the team's purpose, strategy and goals. So, in the team you need to be on the same page and heading in the same direction. In teams, although the individual is clearly important, it has to be about the *us* as well as the *me*.

CONTEXT

Context is about the wider climate in which both the team and individuals operate. It is essential to create a culture and climate that encourages and supports the goals of the team. Former England Rugby Head Coach Stuart Lancaster used to say that culture precedes performance (Personal communication with authors, 2018). And he was partly right! If the culture is poor – it will affect the team's performance – as we have often seen.

But the opposite isn't necessarily true! Even if you create a good culture, it doesn't necessarily create good performance. In order to create better performance, the most successful sports team on the planet – the New Zealand All Blacks rugby team – did have to address the culture of their team when a number of their players were in trouble for off-field demeanours. The critical question is, does the culture get in the way of effective performance? If the answer is yes, then it needs to be addressed. This is the same in business as it is in sports organisations. The team leader needs to reflect on the existing culture within his or her team and create the appropriate cultural climate in order for the team to perform effectively.

PROCESS

This is about developing a cohesive team and the processes that can be used to do this. There are three subcomponents of Process.

- Relays
- Relationships
- Shared purpose.

Relays. One of the processes is to be able to use senior members of the team to act as a relay. If the team is a large one, then you cannot realistically know what's going on with every member. However, the team members themselves can and do know what is going on. If you are able to have a subgroup of senior team members who are in tune with your vision and approach, then they can act as substitute team managers and coaches. They can do this by reminding team members of the team goals, values and ways of working and by reinforcing the key messages. This is common in highly effective teams in the world of sport.

For example, the former Liverpool Football Club and Scotland footballer Graeme Souness agrees that the idea of having the senior members of a team act as a sort of relay is critical.

As a team coach you cannot do everything. Unless you have your highly respected members of the team relaying your approach, it will be difficult to manage the team effectively. The highly successful New Zealand rugby team, the All Blacks, with a win ratio of 85 per cent, also use this idea. They have a leadership group within the team, composed of the captain, senior players and also younger players so that the group is fully represented. These people role model and embed the values on a day-to-day basis. The point is that the coach him or herself is not enough. Some sports teams have even appointed co-captains who share the leadership responsibilities and decision making on the field.

REFLECTION

Looking at your team – who are the team members who are respected by the other team members and who can and will relay your message? This is even more important when the team is dispersed geographically or working virtually.

Relationships. Another important aspect a team coach needs to examine is the relationships between team members. For example, what is the level of trust between team members? What are the differences between team members, for example, what differences in ways of working, ages and expectations? What is the level of trust between you and the team and between team members themselves? If the team members don't trust or respect their coach or manager, why would they bother listening to you?

You may like to instigate a conversation with your team about trust. Explore what you all mean by trust, how much trust exists within the group and between each other including their level of trust for you. You can then explore how trust can be further developed in the team. See Chapter 9 for more on trust.

Shared purpose. It's critically important to have conversations with the team about shared purpose. This is not something that can just be assumed. There needs to be absolute clarity around that shared purpose. What does the team want and how will it get there? As a team coach it's your job to initiate and facilitate these conversations. If you don't do this, then you are likely to find that despite talented individuals the team is always going to be less than the sum of its parts. In fact, you may find that the different individuals are working at cross-purpose to each other and actually sabotaging what you are trying to achieve. We wrote more extensively about creating purpose in Chapter 11.

CONTACT

Contact is about managing individual talent. Although we are talking about coaching teams, we can't lose sight of the fact that the team is composed of individuals, and so paradoxically perhaps, we need to be able to address the individual needs, issues, preferences and talents in the team. It is important not to lose sight of the individual and their unique personality traits and personal circumstances. While traditionally the focus of coaching was always about the team, the reality and complexity of modern group settings and squads require a leader to both skilfully coach the team and actively connect to the individual team player. Dave Brailsford, one of the most successful managers/coaches in British/World Cycling, formerly boss of British Cycling and Team Sky (now Team Ineos), calls this a 'rider centred approach'.

At the same time, we need to be aware of team goals and any potential clashes between individual goals and team goals. As a coach you need to be flexible to individual needs within the team and be able to adapt your style to the needs of the team members. There is a popular saying *'There is no I in a team',* and this has been widely accepted, but it is wrong. The team is made up of individuals with their own styles and preferences. The challenge is to recognise these while at the same time building an overall team culture. You have to address both the individual components of the team as well as the team itself; otherwise, the team will not function effectively.

SPECIFIC ASPECTS AND DISCIPLINES OF TEAM COACHING

Professor Peter Hawkins of Henley Business School has developed a useful and practical model focusing on three aspects of team coaching and five disciplines of team coaching (Hawkins, 2021). At the heart of the model are three essential aspects of the team.

1. **Task** – this is the purpose of the team. What it is supposed to do.

2. **Process** – this is *how* the team will achieve its purpose.

3. **Relationships** – these are looked at from two different perspectives: the internal and external relationships that the team has.

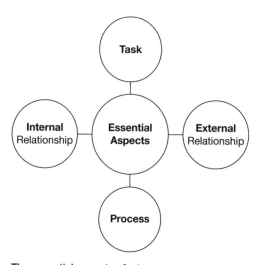

The essential aspects of a team

Professor Hawkins has also developed five key disciplines around these three aspects.

1. Commissioning
2. Clarifying
3. Co-creating
4. Connecting
5. Core learning.

For each of the five disciplines there are some useful questions you can ask when coaching a team. You can use these questions as a basis for developing your team's capabilities and understanding.

- **Commissioning.** What does the team serve? What is its purpose? Why does it exist? How does this align with the organisation objectives?

- **Clarifying.** What is its collective task? What are the core objectives? Is the team clear about roles? Preferences? Is the team clear about working processes?

- **Co-creating.** How is the team working together? How creative is it? How skilled is it at working together? How does it partner internally? How does it manage team dynamics?

- **Connecting.** How does the team partner with the wider organisational system and your key stakeholders?

- **Core learning.** How does the team learn? How does it continue to learn? How does it develop as a team?

We suggest that you can use these questions, together with your own personalised questions, to help create better awareness of the essentials of your team's performance in the context in which you are operating.

CHALLENGES OF TEAM COACHING

We would suggest that team coaching can be more challenging than coaching individuals, as there are more variables to consider and so many different personalities. The biggest challenge in the workplace is often that it seems easier to fall into the trap of telling someone what to do, rather than encourage them to work it out for themselves. On the sports field, as in business, the players/team members have to do it themselves, so just telling them is not enough – you can't do it for them. Coaches are often standing on the sidelines or sitting in their office and must trust that those tasked with making decisions when the pressure is on make the right move. If they make the wrong decision then the coach should review and question their own effectiveness rather than blame others.

Often coaches impose their vision and their way of doing things, so the input of the player or team member is minimal, and they have no ownership. The key for the team coach might be that when team members make their own decisions, they are more valuable, and people feel more committed to them. Perhaps as a team coach, your job then is to firstly find out what the team member is thinking, what they want, what they do best and find ways of releasing that, rather than imposing your own way. In other words, you will be facilitating the process of self-discovery.

A major challenge is actually finding time to coach the team. Our belief is that coaching is a vital process for success. It isn't easy but time spent coaching your team and the individuals in it will be time well spent. In business there often doesn't seem to be any time to practice (as you would do in sport), because in business all the focus is on the next deadline, the next deal, or the next meeting. So, make sure that coaching is part of the team culture. To achieve this, try to role model coaching as part of your own leadership approach. Encourage team members to coach each other in order to make best use of their own skills and capabilities. Build coaching into your regular meetings and discussions. Allocate specific times in your diary for coaching conversations. Reward behaviours that are compatible with a coaching approach.

CHAPTER 14

UNDERSTANDING CHANGE

'No person ever steps in the same river twice.'

Heraclitus of Ephesus, Greek philosopher

INTRODUCTION

Stephen Josephs and Bill Joiner in their excellent book, *Leadership Agility* (2007), predicted that the '*pace of change will continue to increase, and the level of complexity and interdependence will grow*'. As we wrote this in 2021 the world was still in the grip of the Covid 19 pandemic and change and complexity were our constant companions. On the micro level of teams, teams are constantly being created, merged and re-structured to achieve their goals. Even in 2022 as Covid seems to be lessening its grip, many teams are still using 'virtual' meetings on Zoom, Teams or other platforms and meeting face to face less than before. Effective teams evolve and develop to try to become more successful. The world of teams is a world of change.

While a good deal of effort and much work goes into the planning and design of change initiatives, relatively few people see change as a wholly good thing. Typically, senior teams and leaders plan a change process as an opportunity, but it is much harder to convey this to staff, who are more likely to see these planned changes as a threat. Frequently, senior teams overlook the importance of keeping everyone aligned with change throughout the process.

That said, what seems to happen is that senior teams spend a lot of time and effort envisioning, planning and organising a change they intend to introduce into the organisation or team. This often takes place behind closed doors – in board rooms, working parties or project groups. While this goes on, the rest of the organisation has a 'gut' feel that something is going on, and they may even catch snatches of information here and there but actually know very little. This can lead to frustration at best and suspicion at worst. Once the senior team have explored and decided on the way ahead, they may then involve the next level of management. At this stage, often due to excitement about and commitment to the change they have planned, the senior team do not allow sufficient time nor are they open to much further discussion or exploration about the change. So, the next-level managers and other staff can feel disenfranchised and cynical.

Time is now progressing, and the senior team become more committed to and excited about the change, and want to involve the rest of the staff, often using town hall meetings, workshops and many other communication approaches. But what is forgotten is that while the senior team have been working on this for some time, it is completely new to the bulk of the organisation and they feel uninvolved, isolated and resistant.

RESISTANCE TO CHANGE

People respond to change in different ways and for different reasons. Our response is often emotional and can be due to how the change is introduced and initiated. Organisations and leaders tend to focus on the practical and technical context of change rather than engaging with the emotional elements of change.

Some of the most common reasons for resistance to change are:

- fear of the unknown
- little or no understanding about the change
- feelings of insecurity
- little or no buy-in to the change
- self-interest – in that the change negatively affects you.

Whatever the reasons for resistance, many of them can be mitigated against if the change is communicated early, people have the opportunity to contribute in some way and are given the opportunity to buy into the change during the process.

There are several different ways of addressing change within the team. We would like to focus specifically on how teams can use two processes that will help them address change more effectively. We have used these processes successfully with teams ranging from the boardroom to high-performance sports teams.

These approaches are

- The Transition Model of Change

And

- The Four Rooms of Change®

Both these processes will help you to understand people's psychological response and approach to change as well as introducing ideas for effective change management.

THE TRANSITION MODEL OF CHANGE

This model of change was originally developed by William Bridges in 1988. Its main focus is the transitions people go through specifically in relation to the personal and human sides of change – in other words the psychological elements of change. Bridges identified three phases of transition, which are illustrated in the model below (Bridges, 2009):

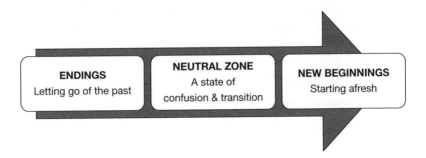

| ENDINGS
Letting go of the past | NEUTRAL ZONE
A state of
confusion & transition | NEW BEGINNINGS
Starting afresh |

This model of change has a lovely simplicity about it and helps teams, team leaders and individuals to understand more about the process they are going through, and the feelings they have about change in general and about any change they are currently experiencing. It helps us to understand the transitions or movement we experience internally while experiencing any change. Bridges suggested that each of these stages needs to be experienced in turn before starting afresh. Let's examine what happens in each of the phases.

- **Endings.** These are all about letting go of the past. Typically, people feel a variety of emotions at this stage – uncertainty, shock, fear, frustration, ambivalence and even anger. And, you might be asking yourself a range of questions, for instance – why the change is necessary, why we are affected, why we didn't know about the change, how is it going to affect me/us? All of this is natural when experiencing change as by definition you are having to let go of something and adapt to something new.

- **Neutral.** In this phase people tend to feel confused, stressed and generally in a state of flux. The old has gone but you don't yet fully understand the way ahead and how the change will affect the team.

- **New Beginnings.** People begin to feel excitement, enthusiasm, relief and acceptance. People begin to buy in and connect with the new reality. They feel a sense of purpose, understand the big picture, know what the plan is and what their role is as a result of the change.

In this model there is an assumption that change results from several transition steps that are more cyclical than linear, that change has to be 'cultivated' rather than forced, and that change is only really achievable through a well-managed transition process. It also acknowledges the complexity of organisations in terms of individuals' and organisational needs and that change needs both a bottom-up and top-down approach. It also specifies the role of managers/leaders as 'facilitators' and it encourages a holistic approach to individual transitions. This latter point implies that not everyone can adapt in the same way to the change and at the same speed.

The point of this model is that real change can only be achieved after going through the three key major phases – Endings/Transition/New Beginnings. Unless each key phase of Transition occurs, change will not actually happen. The failure to identify and be ready for the endings and losses that change produces can be fatal to the change process. One of the main problems we see in teams and organisations is that most organisations try to start with the beginning rather than finishing with it, and we are aware of how paradoxical that sounds!

Here are some tips for each of the phases.

In *Endings*:

- Listen carefully to what people are saying.
- Help people let go of the past.
- Allow time for people to get over what they are losing.
- Acknowledge these losses.
- Mark endings symbolically.
- Make continuities clear – not everything is ending, but it can feel like it to people undergoing change. It's your job to help point out what is NOT changing.

In *Transition*:

- Normalise it by making it clear that this is a normal part of the change process.
- Create temporary structures and roles during the transition period. This helps with agility and flexibility.
- Protect people from failure.
- Have a series of check points so that you know where you are.
- Encourage experiments and creativity. This is the time to try out new ways of doing things.

In *New Beginnings*:

- Visualise the new identity by creating a narrative to share about the new way ahead.

- Redesign roles collaboratively.
- Provide support and training.
- Look for and create quick successes and celebrate them.

REFLECTION

In order to understand these transitions more clearly you might like to reflect about your own experience of change. Use the chart below to explore two different major changes that have affected your life – one change that worked out well and another that didn't.

Questions to ask	Positive Change	Ineffective Change
What has ended in your work life because of this change?		
What feelings did you experience because of this?		
What helped or hindered this process?		
What contributed to the outcome?		

This reflection about your own change experience will help you understand what works and what doesn't for communicating and implementing change.

Typically, some of the key components of good change practice include:

- Communicating about the need for the change frequently and early.
- Allowing people involved to talk about their feelings and emotions in relation to the change.
- Support those involved in the change by listening and exploring ideas with them.
- Enable experimentation by encouraging all those involved to offer up ideas for exploration.

It is also worth noting that we all experience these transitions differently and move through the process at different speeds.

THE FOUR ROOMS OF CHANGE

The other theory we want to explore with you is Claes Janssen's the Four Rooms of Change model. It offers a psychological theory of individuals moving through four stages during any change process. These stages are:

- Contentment
- Denial/Self-censorship
- Confusion
- Inspiration/Renewal.

More recently Janssen has worked with A&L Partners AB and Fyrarummaren AB to develop a series of practical analytical instruments and tools that help individuals and organisations to improve their productivity, leadership, self-awareness and to manage change effectively. Nigel used the Four Rooms Model when he was head coach of Gloucester Rugby, who were a top four team with great players but not delivering on their potential. Everyone was frustrated, their owner, the players and the fans. Their purpose was clear – to win trophies – but they didn't know how. When Nigel explained the Four Rooms of Change it was a game changer and a great example of how theory could be adapted to make it more user friendly and effectively drive team change. It provided him with an opportunity to assess where his team was in terms of their development, but also provided him with an opportunity to see where the team thought they were. Often the team members and team leader have different perspectives of where the team is in the change process.

The Four Rooms of Change model helps both individuals and organisations (including teams) to understand their relationship with change and how they navigate their way through it. It is also suggested that movement through the process at the individual level can only be achieved by passing through each stage in sequence and in an anti-clockwise direction. The illustration below shows the Four Rooms of Change model.

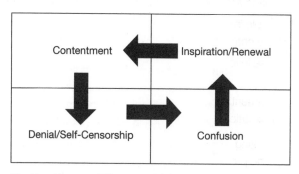

The Four Rooms of Change model

Let's look first of all at individual change. The challenge for individuals is to understand that there is an inevitable slide out of contentment into self-censorship and denial. We are doing well at work for example. We then inevitably get a bit complacent, perhaps prepare a bit less, make less effort, and then we start to get less positive feedback. But we easily go into denial here. We don't want to fully accept what's happening and so we might blame the client or our colleagues – saying that they don't really understand. But then we are called up for a formal review where hard facts and data about our performance are given to us, and we cannot stay in denial any longer. However, the next stage in the change journey is to enter the room of Confusion. This is somewhat paradoxical as we might expect that once we have finally accepted Reality we might move directly to Inspiration/Renewal. Unfortunately, according to Janssen this is not how it works. The next stage in the psychological journey of change is to enter the Confusion room. This is where we have to take stock of our performance – having accepted the new reality – let go of our previous behaviours and get help and support or coaching and mentoring. Once you have accepted the reality of what is happening and gone through the process of admitting what's happened and adjusting to the new reality – perhaps making some changes in your attitudes and behaviours – then you might progress to Inspiration/Renewal.

Once you are in the Inspiration/Renewal room the challenge is to stay there as long as possible, because inevitably you will eventually slide back into Contentment. It's ok to be in contentment – that is where things are calm and enjoyable and productive. But of course, things can get too comfortable and the danger is we become complacent and then slip once more into complacency and denial. Another critical aspect of this concept is that teams tend not to go directly from Contentment into Inspiration/Renewal but will go through the change journey – into denial and confusion – before making it back into Inspiration/Renewal.

When planning a journey, the first step is maybe agreeing where you want to go, the second step is to work out where you are now! When using the Four Rooms of Change model, the destination is the Inspiration/Renewal room; if you are already there, great, if not, which room are you in? The table below sets out some simple descriptors of what life is like and what people say, see and hear when in each room, and will help you identify which room you are in. It is important to remember that you may be in different rooms at different times in different situations and contexts.

You might be in contentment in your family life and in confusion at work for example.

Contentment Room	Inspiration/Renewal Room
■ We are the best/unbeatable	■ Let's make it happen
■ Market leaders	■ We can do this
■ Successful	■ Raise the bar
■ We know our customers	■ I know what our purpose is
■ We have a great track record	■ We're stronger together
■ We're the most profitable	■ We trust each other
■ If it ain't broke, don't fix it	
Denial/Self-Censorship Room	**Confusion Room**
■ Problem? What problem?	■ How did we get in this mess?
■ It's just a trend	■ Let's hire consultants to sort it out.
■ We always do it this way!	■ What's happening?
■ Our staff are no good	■ What have I done wrong?
■ It's only a short-term issue	■ We did that years ago
■ We'll play our way through it	■ Help!

THE CHANGE PROCESS – MOVING ROUND THE FOUR ROOMS

When organisations and teams are successful, they can easily slip from Inspiration/Renewal into the Contentment room. They see themselves as winners, enjoying being on top and don't see that they can be knocked off their 'perch'. These thoughts are often reinforced by everyone around them who are sharing in their success. In this instance, it is extremely difficult to explain that a downturn in recent results is anything more than a trend or a blip and that normal service will soon be resumed. The problem with the Contentment room is that it's a nice place to be and if we're not careful the team will slip into denial. Mike once did some consulting for an organisation that was having some difficulties. What was interesting was that they still had three different restaurants – one with silver service – a shop selling their products at reduced prices to employees, three tennis courts, a bowling club, swimming pool and sports field and, of course, a sun deck with loungers where you could take coffee after lunch! So, they were slipping into Denial. The reality was that they were not doing well but very few people in the organisation were able and willing to accept that reality. When Mike asked managers about their knowledge of their financial difficulties, he was mostly met with a combination of responses that ranged from denial that anything was wrong to outright hostility to changing anything.

In this instance it is about moving people on from Denial and Self-censorship. In order to move people out of Denial/Self-censorship it may be necessary to shock people out of Complacency. You'll need to benchmark performance, break up teams, re-define performance indicators, challenge assumptions, challenge arrogant behaviour, and generally call things out. You'll need to use a fairly confident and direct style here and you'll probably want to do some background research and be confident of the numbers involved.

There is no reason to stay in the Denial/Self-censorship room for any length of time. Once people accept that something needs to change you are heading in the right direction. But of course, it can be hard to get people to accept that they are in Denial/Self-censorship because psychologically it's a difficult place to be. What helps here is if you have created a culture of feedback in your team or organisation – like our example of the English rugby referees that we write about in Chapter 12. If you have created that culture then although there will be moments where people slip into denial/self-censorship, it will not last for very long.

Now that people are listening and accepting the need to make changes, you can continue to benchmark, communicate results, respect the past, avoid blame and start looking to the future. There is no need to offer detailed solutions at this point; all you need is an understanding and acceptance that there is a problem, and something has to change.

Moving from Confusion to Inspiration/Renewal. Now it is time to look forward together, re-set the purpose and overall direction together. It is important to allow team members to provide input and help shape the future at this stage. This is the time to listen carefully to team members, support them while things are unclear and focus on concrete, achievable first steps. It's ok NOT to know the answers here but it is important to allow space for people to reflect and learn while they are in the Confusion room. Make sure you recognise and reward any positive behavioural change – you are looking for small steps in the right direction here – provide fast feedback on results and create momentum for the new direction. Improve the working environment, respect the past, but don't slip into old habits.

Staying in Inspiration/Renewal. Once you arrive in the Inspiration/Renewal room, people now understand the need for the change, they are energised and looking forward to the future. It's the room you need to be in as a team/organisation and a room you want to stay in for as long as possible. It is important that new behaviours are embedded and that there is no 'slippage' into old habits. To achieve this, you must keep raising the bar, to never be happy with the current levels of performance and always striving to improve. You can achieve this through ongoing benchmarking, encouraging individual learning and development and challenging everyone to improve. It's also important to focus on the soft skills too. Learn to be supportive and appreciative and have some fun. World-class performers, coaches, artists and teams are never happy with their performance and are always striving to improve and stay at the top. But the best teams also have fun and recognise that it's important to support and care for each other.

HOW THIS WORKS FOR A TEAM

The Four Rooms theory works a bit differently when it comes to teams and organisations. What happens here is that Inspiration/Renewal and Contentment are linked and so are Denial and Confusion. You can think of it as being mostly on the top floor or mostly on the bottom floor. In most teams there are people in every one of the four rooms at any one point in time. Ideally most people will be on the top floor in Inspiration/Renewal or Contentment, but you still have to address the issue that some people are perhaps stuck on the bottom floor in Denial and/or Confusion. If most people are on the top floor, then it will be much easier to accept change. On the other hand, if most people in the team are on the bottom floor then there is some work to be done before any changes will be effective.

So, when a team is in Contentment then Inspiration/Renewal is also likely to be high and vice versa. If Inspiration/Renewal is high in the team or organisation so is Contentment. In that case then Denial and Confusion will be correspondingly low, as in the graph in Example 1 on the next page.

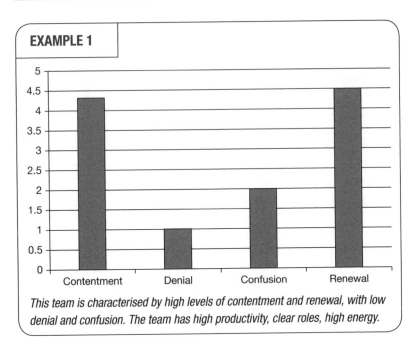

EXAMPLE 1

This team is characterised by high levels of contentment and renewal, with low denial and confusion. The team has high productivity, clear roles, high energy.

But if a team or organisation finds itself in denial then confusion will also be high and vice versa. In this case then you will likely find that contentment and renewal are correspondingly low as in Example 2 below.

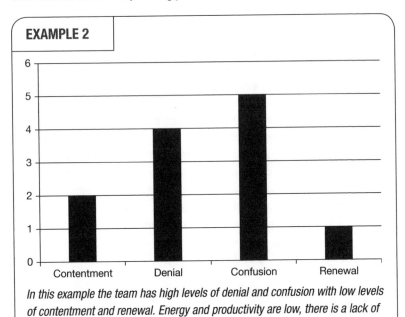

EXAMPLE 2

In this example the team has high levels of denial and confusion with low levels of contentment and renewal. Energy and productivity are low, there is a lack of direction and purpose and a high degree of uncertainty in the team.

EXERCISE

One of the most effective ways of addressing issues in the team is for the team to look at the model and ask themselves what is happening in each of the rooms. If you map out the four rooms on the floor, then the team members can stand in the rooms they feel the team is in at that moment in time. You then ask team members three key questions:

1. *Describe what kind of things are happening, what are the behaviours etc.*
2. *How do we feel about this?*
3. *What can we do about it?*

So, you can start to discuss and resolve the issues as a team without necessarily having an external consultant come in. The aim is to have the team spending most of the time in Contentment and Inspiration/Renewal and to get them out of denial and confusion. However, all teams and organisations are likely to spend some time in these rooms. The critical thing is to make sure there is openness, exploration, honesty and lack of judgemental criticism.

FOUR ROOMS OF CHANGE IN ACTION

Nigel, Mike and Fiona have all used the Four Rooms of Change concept with both sports and business teams and have developed a process that they have successfully implemented over the years. This process is a great starting point and can be used when working with new teams to work out where the team think they are in relation to the four rooms. Of course, all team members are unlikely to be in the same room at the same time. The challenge is getting everyone into the Inspiration/Renewal room and keeping them there.

The process involves the following:

- Present the concept of the Four Rooms of Change and the opportunity it presents for the team to assess where they think they are now and what we need to do to take a positive step forward together.

- Once the team understands the concept, mark out on the floor a cross with masking tape depicting the four rooms, and label each of the four rooms using a card.

- Ask the team to go and stand in the room that they think the team is currently in.

- Once the team have chosen their rooms, this is a good time for the team leader to ask:
  - Why did you choose the room you are in?
  - For those not in the Inspiration/Renewal room, what would it take to move you to the next room?
- The team can then debate and agree which room the team is currently in and what needs to be done to move it to Inspiration/Renewal.
- They then collect the key points discussed and agree on actions required to move forward together.

As the team move forward, it is then easier to discuss where the team are in regard to their performance using the dialogue presented in the Four Rooms of Change model. Working with individuals, teams and organisations it becomes very easy to work out where people are and what they need to do to move to the Inspiration/Renewal room.

TIMING

The question of timing is often raised during these sessions: how long will it take to get us into the Inspiration/Renewal room, and do we have time? The key to progress is recognition of the need to change; once that is accepted, organisations, people and teams can move. For example, a team can move from Contentment to Denial and into Confusion in an instant. It is the realisation that there is a problem and it needs to be fixed that creates the movement.

In the Confusion room, there are a number of challenges: too much debate and no agreed way forward will result in paralysis. The challenges of the Four Rooms of Change are therefore not so much linked to time, but rather a recognition of the need to change, then a willingness to change and the ability to work together to create the right strategy and processes to enter the Inspiration/Renewal room.

> '*The Inspiration/Renewal room is the place to be*' says Nigel. '*I was invited to run a coaching session for the England Rugby World Cup team in 2003 before they left for Australia. I arrived at Penny Hill Park, the team's training base and spent the afternoon with the coaches and players. I was blown away by the environment that Clive Woodward and his team had created. It was a hive of activity, everyone was clearly focussed and working hard, the team looked in amazing physical condition and there was an air of quiet confidence around*

the place. It was an environment where you felt nothing is impossible,
something special. I remember driving away from Penny Hill that
afternoon thinking, England will win the Rugby World Cup – they are all
in the Inspiration/Renewal room'.

Some months later, having won the World Cup and returned to scenes
never witnessed in English rugby before, the team failed to repeat the
standards they had achieved in Australia that summer. The team most
likely slipped out of the Contentment room into Denial and Confusion before
eventually slowly making their way back into Inspiration/Renewal.

What room is your favourite football team, political party, business team
or indeed are you currently living in? If they or you are not in the Inspira-
tion/Renewal or Contentment rooms, what do you think it would take to
get you/them there and to stay there as long as possible without slipping
into Denial?

The philosopher Sir Karl Popper said that all things are insecure and
in a state of flux and teams are no exception to this rule (Popper, 2002).
Since change is constant, no person or team can live forever in the Inspira-
tion/Renewal room. Inevitably teams who are doing well (in the Inspiration/
Renewal and Contentment rooms in this model) become complacent and
then slip into the Denial or Self-censorship room. We have seen that teams
in Denial usually have people in Confusion as well and it is not possible to
jump straight back into Inspiration/Renewal and Contentment. The team
must actively address the issues in the ways we have described above.

They can then start to reassess things, ask difficult questions, and learn
new things. Only when they have had a chance to reassess and change
attitudes and behaviours is there a chance for the team to move on to
Inspiration/Renewal and Contentment.

As we mentioned earlier in the chapter – teams can spend longer or
shorter times in each room. In fact, teams and organisations can get stuck
in Contentment, Denial or Confusion, and even die there. The goal is to stay
as long as possible in Inspiration/Renewal and Contentment (the highly productive rooms) and as short a time as possible in Denial and Confusion. (To
learn more about the theory, models, or to become a certified user contact
info@fourrooms.com or drusilla.copeland@fourrooms.com)

Finally, when your team is in a period of change it is important to ensure
that:

■ the team move through the process together though they may not
be at the same stage in their psychological journey, which means
flexibility is necessary

- communication begins early
- there is clarity about the vision, goals and purpose of the change
- everyone is committed to the change and the process they have to go through
- all involved recognise that the change is in service of and of value to the business of the organisation.

CHAPTER 15

USING FACILITATION SKILLS TO INCREASE PERFORMANCE

'The degree to which I can create relationships, which facilitate the
growth of others as separate persons, is a measure of the growth
I have achieved in myself.'

Carl Rogers, American psychologist and author

WHAT DO WE MEAN BY FACILITATION?

Let us say up front that we believe that all team members should have the necessary skills and experience to adopt the facilitator role.

To facilitate the team is to be a change agent and help the team to develop and improve performance. The facilitator will also help the individuals in the team to develop and improve their own performance, but as a team facilitator they will be focusing on how the individuals contribute to the team. The term first came to prominence with the development of quality circles in the 1970s. It was found that these teams of people needed someone to facilitate the process of coming up with improvements. So the facilitator didn't solve the problems but helped the members of the quality circle to have the means and processes to solve the issues. The word facilitator comes from the Latin word *facilis*, which means 'easy', so the facilitator is literally there to make things easy for the team to work together.

You may want to get some training on how to be an effective facilitator, but you can also learn on the job as long as you are prepared to ask for and accept feedback on your performance. It is our strong belief that you as a team leader or team member should learn the skills of facilitation, and if you are already a good facilitator, be prepared to develop your colleagues in these skills so that everyone in the team can act as a facilitator.

WHY DO WE NEED TO FACILITATE THE TEAM?

What often happens in teams is that there is a clear focus towards action and finding the answers to the problems. Unfortunately, just being focused on solving problems doesn't necessarily make the team any better at actually solving these issues.

So, a facilitator looks at three key things in the team: The WHAT, the HOW and the WHO.

- The WHAT is the work the team are engaged in – in other words the task.
- The HOW is the process of accomplishing that task.
- The WHO consists of the relationships and dynamics between the team members.

The most important are the HOW and the WHO because they are instrumental in defining how the task gets done and whether it is done effectively.

Teams often focus on the people but overlook the *process* of how the team is working, because the problems faced by teams are mostly linked to the process of how they work together. The facilitator will specifically look at these processes and make the team aware of HOW they work together.

What are these processes? Well, one good example is listening. Do the team members actually listen to each other, or are they constantly interrupting each other? Clearly a team that doesn't listen to its own members cannot be very effective! Another example might be inclusion. Who is included in the conversations? Is one person dominating? Does everyone get a fair chance to speak up? Are some members being denied the opportunity to speak? Are some too shy to contribute?

What about trust? Do the team members trust each other? Clearly if there is a lack of trust in the team it will not be as effective as it could be. Who has the most influence? Where do they get that influence from? Is it because they are the most experienced person? Or simply the most powerful? Or just the person who shouts the loudest? Just because they have influence doesn't mean they are right!

We frequently run experiential exercises for teams during our training sessions at Hult International Business School. What often happens is that when faced with a problem to solve, a couple of extraverted members come up with some ideas and are not shy about expressing them. These then get tried out but don't actually work. What no one has bothered to do is ask the quietest, most introverted member of the group, who hasn't said a word yet, what he or she actually thinks. Very often it's their idea which turns out to be the best one. Will the team address these issues if left to its own devices? Our experience is that it will not. It is more likely the team will focus on getting things done and they do not always have the experience or capability to address the kind of issues being talked about. This is where someone with excellent facilitation skills will bring a competitive advantage to the team.

An example is a team of managers Mike worked with in Sweden. The team was set up as a project group to come up with solutions to some of the strategic issues faced by the firm. Although all the members were managers and quite experienced, they did not appear to have much knowledge about the basics of teamwork and worked rather slowly together. There was a lack of creative and strategic thinking. They were all very hard working, were extremely cooperative and showed a high degree of willingness but did not appear to be able to stand back and reflect and view the project from many different angles. They did not have much practice in building on each other or facilitating the team. They were very action oriented, extremely

practical and pragmatic, but not so strong on conceptual, strategic or creative thinking. They were also very strong on technical issues but had rather
a lot to learn about group and team dynamics, communication and people
management in general. In short, they did not demonstrate effective interpersonal and facilitation skills.

We could describe many of the teams we work with in this way, that
is, technically strong, pleasant and cooperative, willing, practically minded,
hardworking and oriented towards results. But these undoubted qualities
are not sufficient to make an effective team. These managers need to be
able to facilitate the team to work more effectively together.

WHAT SKILLS DOES A FACILITATOR NEED?

We include a non-exhaustive list of the kind of skills a facilitator will need in
order to facilitate team processes effectively:

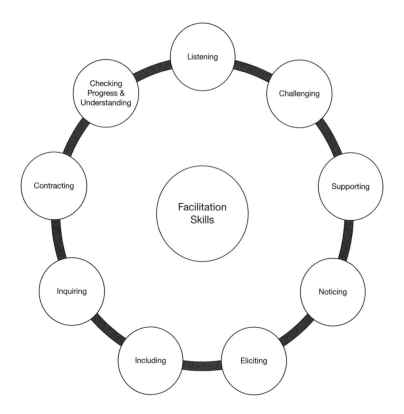

- **Listening.** A facilitator must be an effective listener, who can listen at several levels. By that we mean listening to the obvious things such as the facts but also being able to listen more closely to the emotions and what is not being said.

- **Challenging.** There are times when the facilitator will need to be able to challenge team members, and there is a real skill to challenging effectively. Getting the balance right between challenging and supporting is difficult and the challenge has to be made in a skilful way. That means the facilitator challenging the idea rather than the person and doing it in a way that does not antagonise the team. Poor challenges are often judgmental and criticise the person or team directly.

- **Supporting.** The team facilitator's main role is to support and encourage the team to work well together. So encouraging, appreciating and supporting both the team and individual team members is an important skill. As a rule of thumb, a good facilitator will tend to use more positive and supportive behaviours than judgemental and critical ones.

- **Noticing.** What we mean here is that the facilitator has to notice what is going on in the team. What is the atmosphere like? What are the undercurrents? What are the emotions in the team? One way of picking up on emotions is to be aware of the non-verbal communication in the team. What is the body language? What kind of tone and language are team members using with each other? Professor Albert Meharabian estimated that when the subject was an emotional one, up to 93 per cent of any communication could be non-verbal (Meharabian, 2007).

- **Eliciting.** The ability to create trust and bring out what a person really thinks. This means encouraging people to come forward and to speak up openly and honestly.

- **Including.** Inclusion is one of the fundamental human needs and the team facilitator needs to be careful to make sure that everyone has a voice in the team. It's so easy for certain team members to dominate a conversation. They may be highly extrovert or more confident than others, or they may simply like the sound of their own voice, but the facilitator has to intervene and make sure that everyone is able to speak up, and that no one person or group dominates the conversation. Another thing he/she needs to look out for are people interrupting each other. There is really no excuse for people interrupting someone else. If a person is going on too long or being too long winded, then you as facilitator have the right to intervene and ask them to get to the point. One process that works well is to allow someone to speak for say, three minutes uninterrupted, before allowing others to question or challenge.

- **Inquiring.** This is similar to eliciting information but is all about asking good and open questions together with effective listening. The skill here is to be able to ask and probe, without making judgements on the responses. This is more difficult than it sounds as we often observe team leaders asking too many closed questions, or not probing deeply enough into an issue, or worse still, making critical remarks.

- **Contracting.** It's important for the facilitator to contract with the team so that everyone is clear about the purpose and process of the team meeting. This covers the essentials like timing but also issues such as confidentiality and what kind of behaviours are desirable, and which are not acceptable to the team. As an example, the facilitator might agree with the team what the protocol should be around using mobile devices.

- **Checking Progress and Understanding.** One of the key roles of the facilitator is to check the team's progress. So, they might pause the proceedings by asking for a 'time out' (often by making the T sign with their two hands as a signal). They would then go round the team asking each person to what extent progress was being made on the issue under discussion, and also by asking what else or what more could be done. It's common for a team meeting to lose focus and go off track so it's the facilitator's job to notice this and help get the team back on track. It's also essential that the facilitator is able to check people's understanding during the meeting. So, they need to constantly listen and observe and be able to notice when there seems to be any confusion or a lack of understanding between team members. One way of doing this is to intervene and then using paraphrasing say something like '*If I understand you correctly John, you are saying ... ?*'. So, you are essentially rephrasing what John has said but in a way that is hopefully clearer to those who haven't grasped John's point. This then allows John to agree or to further clarify his meaning.

WHAT ATTITUDES DOES A FACILITATOR NEED?

There are a number of attitudes that an effective facilitator will display. Again, we offer a non-exhaustive list.

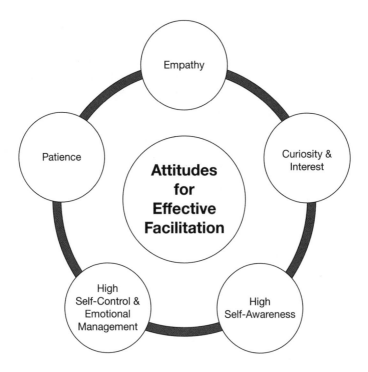

- **Empathy.** It is critical to be empathetic and not to be patronising towards team members. Remember you are acting as the facilitator to enable the team to perform well, not as the dictator.

- **Curiosity and Interest.** A high degree of curiosity is essential to allow you to probe and inquire. You also need to be genuinely interested in both the people and the issue.

- **High Self-awareness.** It's obvious that if you have low self-awareness and have no idea of how you are coming across and being perceived by team members, then you are not going to be an effective facilitator. So it is important that you seek and are receptive to feedback.

- **High Self-control/Emotional Management.** Emotions are often to the fore in team discussions – especially where there are areas of disagreements. The team members themselves may become angry or annoyed and express that, but your job as the facilitator is to keep your own emotions in check so that you can defuse the situation for others.

- **Patience.** Let's be honest here. Facilitating a team isn't easy and you will on occasion require the patience of Job to do it well (referring to the Biblical figure of Job who was famed for his ability to endure trials and tribulations). If you are not naturally a patient person then that is an attitude you will have to work on as many of the issues you are trying to resolve that will be caused by impatient team members.

Finally, you will find that some team members will have many of the necessary skills and should be given the opportunity to practise them and receive feedback to enable them to develop further in this area.

CHAPTER 16

THOUGHTS ON THE FUTURE OF TEAMS

'Companies are recognising the benefits of shifting to a team structure within a unified, inclusive and collaborative workforce – one that enables agility and unites talent to focus on gaining competitive advantage in an evolving marketplace.'

Pulse Survey – Meeting the Challenges of Developing Collaborative Teams for Future Success: Harvard Business Review Analytic Services.

Teams already play a critical role in the success of many organisations and looking ahead this will only become more significant. Recent experience of the worldwide pandemic has provided the impetus for teams to become more adaptable, collaborative and agile to ensure business continuity in many national and global organisations. We believe that in the future we are more likely to have a network of teams to which we belong, that teams will form and disband more frequently and rapidly, and that team members and team leaders will have to develop and adapt their capabilities to deal with all these changes.

Over the past 18 months we have heard many stories from people we have trained, interviewed and coached about how teams have had to face new challenges, solve problems and innovate at speed. Many of these stories have been told to us by people who work in the healthcare sector which has had to operate within a crisis environment due to the pandemic. These stories have been about the significant change from the usual hierarchical approach where teams seemed to work on the same issue for many months before a decision was made and then many more before implementation could take place. What they are now experiencing is the rapid forming of cross-functional teams to deal with the new challenges they face on a day-to-day basis, the speed with which decisions have to be made and implemented and how creative and innovative they had to be to deal with the unprecedented and wicked problems they are encountering.

It is our belief that much of what has happened during the world crisis over recent years must be captured and acted upon to capitalise on the benefits and positive changes and to move ahead towards better team processes for fairer, more efficient, collaborative and agile teams.

The following six themes are the ones we consider to be most relevant when considering how teams will work going forward.

1. **Leadership style and approach.** The world is rapidly changing, and it is simply too important for us to ignore the collective intelligence of the team. This means that the way teams work together and how they are led is set to change radically in the future. Instead of teams having a single leader who is in charge, every single team member will have to develop the ability to both lead and follow. Team leaders and team members will have to develop their skills in areas such as facilitation, feedback processes, influencing, motivation and managing change. Additionally, the ability for teams to learn and adapt on their feet will be vital. Environments are changing rapidly and the capacity of teams to learn new skills and to be flexible needs to keep pace.

2. **Networks of teams.** In the future, it's likely that everyone will have a network of teams to which they belong. Research suggests that already, only 38 per cent of companies are organised by function, so we will see more and more cross-functional, multi-cultural and virtual teams. Teams will be forming and disbanding more rapidly as business needs change. Team leaders will have to develop the ability to create teams, get them performing effectively and then disband them on a positive note. They will also have to be skilful in their ability to collaborate, flex their style and relate to a wide range of people – and to equip their team members to do the same. Team-based rather than individual reward is also becoming more common. This is a highly emotional area that will demand a steep change in attitude and approach and real skill on the part of the leader.

3. **New ways of working.** During the Covid pandemic many of us became used to new ways of working, specifically the use of video technology – typically Microsoft Teams or Zoom. These technologies were in existence long before the pandemic, but what the pandemic did was make it essential that we all became familiar with and users of video conferencing, not only for work but also for keeping in touch with family and friends. This has led to many people now talking about **'hybrid working'** as a way ahead. Hybrid working implies that we will have more choice about how we work – either from home or at the office. We hear stories from our clients about the choices they are being given including: 100 per cent home or office working, a 50-50 balance or some other balance of home and office working. What's for sure is that most of us will have more choice. The keys to success for hybrid working will be getting the balance right for all involved, using technology to its best effect, ensuring that leaders and their teams have the skills and abilities to work well together and that organisations ensure their vision, purpose, values and goals are communicated and understood.

4. **The need for greater diversity and inclusion.** Generation Z and millennial employees play a big part in teams now and more so in the future, so it's important for team leaders to understand how to get the best out of them. Our research shows that Millennials want challenging and interesting work, flexible working patterns and frequent praise. They want informal, friendly relationships with their managers, and for their bosses to share their knowledge and experience with them. They are digital natives who have grown up with technology and expect to be able to use it to its fullest extent in the workplace. Much of this is

alien to team leaders, who have grown up against a more hierarchical, slow-moving backdrop. Trying to force Millennials into what is rapidly becoming an outdated mode is futile. If leaders want to get the best out of their Generation Z and millennial team members, they need to tap into what motivates and engages them.

Additionally, the typical team of the future will be made up not just of different cultures, but also different generations. Demographic changes, coupled with changes in pension legislation, mean that 'Baby Boomer' employees will be working well beyond traditional retirement age. The challenge for team leaders will be to get the generations working together harmoniously. Over-50s will need to adjust to new ways of working, embrace new technologies and come to terms with the fact they may be reporting to people from a less-experienced, younger generation. Millennials will need to focus on developing relational and interpersonal skills so that they can work effectively with older colleagues and learn from their knowledge and experience.

Cross-functional teams and Global teams will also increasingly feature strongly in teams in the future. Cross-functional teams mean that people from different functional expertise will work together and for many of these people they may also be located at different venues throughout the world so they will be not only Cross-functional but also Global. This will mean an even greater need for team members and leaders to be able to show excellent communication skills, be flexible in their behaviour, to work collaboratively towards clear goals, to be organised in their ways of working and to accept difference as positive, worthy of time and effort.

See Chapter 5 for more on diversity and inclusion.

5. **Building engagement, social connection and shared purpose.**
   Engaged teams work more effectively. Research by Gallup shows that engaged employees have 22 per cent higher productivity, 65 per cent lower turnover and 41 per cent fewer defects. Having a strategic vision and being able to translate this into clear objectives is key to success. People need to understand why what they do matters, and how it fits into the bigger picture. Leaders also need to make sure people feel valued and appreciated for their efforts and to show an active interest in team members, their aspirations and what drives them. Teams who are socially connected and have a shared purpose

tend to be most successful, and looking to the future this will become even more vital for both organisational and personal success.

Maggie Alphonsi illustrates this well when she told us that the best team that she ever played for was not her England team, but her club team – Saracens.

The reason I felt they were the best team was because we had lots of time together and we built this emotional bond. We weren't getting paid to be there, we were there because we wanted to be there, to be with our friends. These team mates were becoming almost family to me. And even in that highly successful Saracens team which won Premiership titles, it wasn't necessarily the achievements and accolades that made the team successful. I believe it was because we had a close family-like bond, we spent a lot of time together, we had no real agenda, we were not paid to be there, there were no contracts in amateur women's rugby. You just joined a club and if you didn't like it you left it, so that was probably the best team I have been a part of.

6. **Health and well-being.** It is becoming clear that the health and well-being of all employees contributes to effective performance, especially when performance becomes more and more about high cognitive ability and creativity. Sports teams have recognised this for many years and Nigel tells us that in a typical rugby setting such things as diet and nutrition, sleep, mental health, hydration and exercise are all key elements of success. In the sports setting they employ dieticians, physiotherapists and psychologists to oversee this area and to offer support and guidance. Business organisations could learn a lot from sport in this area, especially in regard to hydration, stress, posture and nutrition. For example, we know of organisations who are offering posture assessments, physiotherapy, counselling and good-quality, free fresh food in their staff restaurants. They realise that people can only perform at a high level if they are supported and cared for as human beings. A good example of an organisation thinking deeply about health and well-being is Bristol Rugby Club who have created a purpose-built high-performance centre that caters to all their players' preparation needs. It also sends an important message to the players that the club values preparation and is prepared to invest in it and in its players. Their director of rugby – former Samoan and All Black international – Pat Lam says

that they want to build a more inclusive culture – so for example the players eat alongside office workers and coaching staff so that everyone connects more easily. Importantly, the Rugby Players Association are also represented at the centre, offering support for injured players and education programmes for academy players and those preparing for post-career opportunities.

The club culture according to Lam (Personal communication with authors, 2021) is based on love and sacrificing for each other. To quote him, *'People love their jobs when they feel valued, appreciated and respected'*. Perhaps teams and organisations need to reflect more deeply about how they connect, how they care for each other and bring in a little bit more love into their culture. The recent EY survey into Empathy in business tells us that 90 per cent of US workers believe that empathetic leadership leads to higher job satisfaction and 79 per cent agree it decreases employee turnover (Ernst & Young, 2021).

In a private interview with the authors in 2022, Maggie Alphonsi explained that a good coach in her opinion is one who doesn't focus on their own ego but focuses on developing the individuals and the team. When we asked her what she was looking for in a leader, she replied:

A leader who is empathetic. By that I mean I want them to understand me and what I have gone through and the challenges that I am having and empathise with that. I think that's very important.

As the examples above illustrate, ultimately it's the investment in people, and care for them as individuals, that drives high-performing teams and success. To paraphrase the great German philosopher Immanuel Kant – *'Don't treat humans as a means to end, but as an end in themselves!'*

REFERENCES AND FURTHER READING

Armstrong, A., Olivier, S. and Wilkinson, S. (2018) *Shades of Grey – An Exploratory Study of Engagement in Work Teams*. Ashridge/Hult International Business School.

Baron, A. (2013) What do engagement measures really mean? *Strategic HR Review*, 12(1), 21–25. https://doi.org/10.1108/14754391311282450

Barrett, R. (2017) *The Values-Driven Organisation: Unleashing Human Potential for Performance and Profit*. Routledge.

Bennis, W. (2009) *On Becoming A Leader*. Basic Books.

Binney, G. *et al.* (2012) *Living Leadership*. Pearson FT series.

Boston Consulting Group (2014) The most innovative companies 2014: Breaking through is hard to do. See https://www.bcg.com/en-gb/publications/collections/most-innovative-companies (accessed 15 February 2022).

Brent, M. and Dent, F.E. (2010) *The Leader's Guide to Influence: How to Use Soft Skills To get Hard Results*. FT Prentice Hall.

Brent, M. and Dent, F.E. (2014) *The Leader's Guide to Managing People: How to Use Soft Skills to Get Hard Results*. FT Publishing.

Brent, M. and Dent, F.E. (2015) *The Leader's Guide to Coaching & Mentoring: How to Use Soft Skills to Get Hard Results*. FT Publishing.

Brent, M. and Dent, F.E. (2017) *The Leadership of Teams: How to Develop and Inspire High-Performance Teamwork*. Bloomsbury.

Brent, M. and McKergow, M. (2009) No more Heroes. *Coaching at Work*, 4(5), 44–48.

Bridges, W. (2009) *Managing Transitions: Making the Most of Change* (3rd edition). Nicolas Brealey.

Burkus, D. (2021) *Leading from Anywhere*. Houghton Mifflin Harcourt Publishing.

Calne, D. (2010) *Within Reason – Rationality and Human Behaviour*. Vintage.

Cone Purpose study (2019) *How to build deeper bonds, amplify the message and expand the customer base*. See 2019 Porter Novelli/Cone Gen Z Purpose Study — Cone Communications | Cone | Cone PR | Cone Inc | PR Agency | Boston | NYC.

Cooperrider, D. *et al.* (2008) *Appreciative Inquiry Handbook: For Leaders of Change* (2nd edition). Berrett-Koehler Publishers.

Covey, S.M.R. (2006) *The Speed of Trust* (with R. Merrill), Free Press.

Covey, S.M.R. (2004) *The 7 Habits of Highly Effective People*. Simon & Schuster.

Csikszentmihalyi, M. (2008) *Flow, The Psychology of Optimal Experience*. Harper.

Curtis, B.R. (2011) *Psychology of Trust*. Nova Science Publishers, Inc.

De Shazer, S. *et al.* (2021) *More than Miracles*: *The State of the Art of Solution Focused Brief Therapy*. Routledge Mental Health Classic.

Deloitte University Press (2016) *Global Human Capital Trends. The New Organisation: Different by Design*. Deloitte University Press.

Deming, W.E., Orsini, J.N. *et al.* (2013) *The Essential Deming*. McGraw Hill.

Dent, F.E. and Brent, M. (2006) *Influencing: Skills and Techniques for Business Success.* Palgrave Macmillan.

DDI Report on Diversity and Inclusion 2020. See https://www.ddiworld.com/research/inclusion-report (accessed 07/11/2021).

Dillon, B. and Bourke, J. (2016) *The Six Signature Traits of Inclusive Leaders. Thriving in a Diverse New World*. Deloitte University Press.

Dimitracopoulos, M. (2020) *Four Ways to Put Your Purpose to Work in 2021*. EY. See https://www.ey.com/en_ae/purpose/four-ways-to-put-your-purpose-to-work (accessed 7/11/2021).

Drawer, S. (2010) *Times,* 17 July 2019.

Duhigg, C. (2016) What Google learned. *N.Y Times Magazine*, 25 February 2016.

Edmondson, A. (2014) *Building A Psychologically Safe Workplace*. Ted talk.

Edmondson, A. (2020) *The Fearless Organisation*. Wiley.

European Institute for Gender Equality (2021) Index score for European Union for the 2021 edition. See eige.europa.eu/gender-equality-index/2021 (accessed 23/02/2022).

Easyjose Coffee. See https://easyjosecoffee.co.uk (accessed 15/11/2021).

Ernst & Young Imperative Study (2019) See https://www.ey.com/en_ae/ growth/ceo-imperative-global-challenges (accessed 7/11/2021).

Ernst & Young Empathy in Business survey (2021) See https://www.ey.com/ en_us/news/2021/09/ey-empathy-in-business-survey (accessed 28/11/2021).

Gallup & Bates College (2019) *Forging Pathways to Purposeful Work: The Role of Higher Education*. See https://www.gallup.com/ education/248222/gallup-bates-purposeful-work-2019.aspx (accessed 7/11/2021).

Gast, A. *et al.* (2020) *Purpose – Shifting from Why to How*. McKinsey. 22 April 2020. See https://www.mckinsey.com/business-functions/ people-and-organizational-performance/our-insights/purpose-shifting- from-why-to-how (accessed 07/11/2021).

Glassdoor Inc. (2014) *What Job Seekers Really Think About Your Diversity and Inclusion Stats*. See https://www.glassdoor.com/employers/blog/ diversity (accessed 15/02/2022).

Goffee, R. and Jones, G. (2019) *Why Should Anyone be Led by You?* HBR Press.

Gottman, J.M. (2011) *The Science of Trust: Emotional Attunement for Couples*. W.W. Norton & Co.

Gray, J.A. (1970) The psychophysiological basis of introversion-extraversion. *Behaviour Research and Therapy*, 8(3), 249–266.

Gray, J.A. (1987) *The Psychology of Fear and Stress*. New York: Cambridge University Press.

Greenleaf, R.K. (2002) *Servant Leadership*. Paulist Press.

Grint, K. (2005) *Leadership – Limits and Possibilities*. Palgrave Macmillan.

Hawkins, P. (2021) *Leadership Team Coaching: Developing Collective Transformational Leadership*. Kogan Page.

Haslam, S.A., Reicher, S.D. and Platow, M.J. (2011) *The New Psychology of Leadership*. Psychology Press.

Hogan, R. (2017) *Personality and The Fate of Organisations* (1st edition). Psychology Press.

Hornstein, H.A., Luss, R. and Parker, W. (2002) Watson Wyatt Human Capital Index. Paper presented at the 2002 International Management Conference, Society for Advancement of Management, McLean, Virginia, 5–8 April 2002.

Hunt, V., Layton, D. and Prince, S. (2015) *Diversity Matters*. McKinsey.

Janssen, C. (2011) *Introduction to the Four Rooms of Change: A Practical Everyday Psychology, Vol. 1*. Ander and Lindström AB (out of print).

Janssen, C. (2012) *Introduction to the Four Rooms of Change*. Fyrarummaren.se

Janssen Claes (2011) *Introduction to the Four Rooms of Change: A Practical Everyday Psychology. Vol. 2 Fifteen More Years of Experiences*. Ander and Lindström AB (out of print).

Josephs, S. and Joiner, W. (2007) *Leadership Agility: Five Levels of Mastery for Anticipating and Initiating Change*. Jossey Bass.

Kahn, W.A. (1990) Psychological conditions of personal engagement and disengagement at work. *Academy of Management Journal,* 33(4), 692–724.

Kahneman, D., Sibony, O. and Sunstein, C. (2021) *Noise: A Flaw in Human Judgement*. Hachette.

Kantar Report (2020) *Purpose 2020 – reigniting purpose led growth*. Kantar.

Kerr, J. (2013) *Legacy: What the All Blacks Can Teach us About the Business of Life*. Constable.

Lencioni, P.M. (2002) *The Five Dysfunctions of a Team*. John Wiley and Sons.

Lewis, R. and Donaldson-Fielder, E. (2014) *Managing for Sustainable Employee Engagement*. CIPD.

MacLeod, D. and Clarke, N. (2009) *Engaging for Success*. BIS.

Maslow, A. (1943) *A Theory of Human Motivation*. General Press.

Maister, D., Green, C.H. and Galford, R.M. (2002) *The Trusted Advisor*. Simon and Schuster.

General McChrystal, S., Silverman, D., Collins, T. and Fussell, C. (2015) *Team of Teams: New Rules of Engagement for a Complex World*. Penguin.

McKergow, M. (2009) Leader as host, host as leader. *International Journal of Leadership in Public Service,* 5(1), 19–24.

McKergow, M. and Bailey, H. (2014) *Host – 6 New Roles of Engagement*. Solutions Books.

Meharabian, A. (2007) *Non-Verbal Communication*. Aldine Transaction.

Neal, S. *et al.* (2021) *Global Leadership Forecast*. DDI.

Parker J. (2017) *A Report into the Ethnic Diversity of UK Boards. The Parker Review Committee*. Final report October 2017.

Parks, S.D. (2005) *Leadership can be Taught*. HBR Press.

Peterson, J.B. (2018) *12 Rules for Life – An Antidote for Chaos*. Allen Lane.

Porter, E.H. (1950) *An Introduction to Therapeutic Counselling*. Houghton Mifflin.

Porter, E.H. (1971, 1996) *Strength Deployment Inventory*. Carlsbad, CA. Personal Strengths Publishing.

PWC (2011) *Millennials at work: Reshaping the workplace*. See https://www.pwc.com/m1/en/services/consulting/documents/millennials-at-work.pdf.

Popper, K. (2002) *The Logic of Scientific Discovery*. Routledge Classics.

Reina, D. and Reina, M. (2015) *Trust and Betrayal in the Workplace. Building Effective Relationships in the Workplace*. EDS Publications.

Reynolds, A. and Lewis, D (2017) Teams solve problems faster when they're more cognitively diverse. *Harvard Business Review,* 30 March 2017.

Reynolds, A., Goddard, J. *et al.* (2020) *What Philosophy Can Teach You About Being a Better Leader*. Kogan Page.

Roberts, K. (2005) *Lovemarks – The Future Beyond Brands*. PowerHouse Books.

Rogers, C.R. (2011) *On Becoming a Person*. Robinson New edition.

Rogers, C.R. (2012) *Client Centred Therapy*. Robinson New edition.

Schein, E. (1996) *Organizational Culture and Leadership* (2nd edition). Jossey Bass.

Schein, E.H. (1992) *How Can Organizations Learn Faster? The Problem of Entering the Green Room*. MIT Sloan School of Management. Spring 1992 wp#3409-92.

Schofield, C.P. (2011) *Great Expectations: Managing Generation Y*. Institute of Leadership and Management /Ashridge Business School.

Schutz, W. (1992) Beyond FIRO-B – three new theory derived measures – element B: Behavior, element F: Feelings, element S: Self. *Psychological Reports*, 70, 915–937.

Schutz, W. (1994) *The Human Element: Productivity, Self-Esteem and the Bottom Line*. San Francisco, CA: Jossey-Bass.

Sinek, S. (2011) *Start with Why. How Great Leaders Inspire Everyone to Take Action*. Penguin.

Sisodia, R. (2014) Quoted in *Business of Purpose*.com See https://www.businessofpurpose.com/statistics (accessed 7/11/21).

Schwarz, S. See https://www.thevaluesproject.com/about-shalom-schwartz/ (accessed 07/11/2021).

Strauss, A. Interview in Forbes magazine. See https://www.forbes.com/sites/daniellerossingh/2019/12/19/qa-former-england-captain-andrew-strauss-talks-cricket-business-and-psychology/?sh=72f4bf8a6b39 (accessed 20/12/2021).

The Guardian, 22 July 2021. Bank of England admits shortcomings in promoting diversity.

Tuckman, B.W. and Jensen, M.A.C. (1977) Stages of small group development revisited. *Group and Organizational Studies* 2, 419–427.

Turner, M. (1996) *The Literary Mind*. Oxford University Press.

Wheately, M. and Frieze, D. (2011) From hero to host. *Resurgence,* 264, 14–17.

Whitmore, J. (2010) *Coaching for Performance: The Principles and Practise of Coaching and Leadership*. Nicolas Brealey.

Winnicott, D. (1971) *Playing and Reality*. Tavistock.

INDEX